'What struck people about the first fol[lowers of Jesus was not that]
they were extraordinary – in fact, t[hey were ordinary,]
untrained men ... (but) they realized th[ey had been with Jesus]
(Acts 4:13). For anyone who believes i[n Jesus Christ, this book]
is a fantastic encouragement to coope[rate with the Spirit in living]
the greatness of His life out from inside you.'
Paul Harcourt, Vicar of All Saints' Woodford Wells, Ambassador for New Wine England

'Henry's many years of pastoral leadership, devotion to discipleship and discipling others shines through. This is a super helpful book and resource for all, no matter how long you've been following the way of Jesus.'
Carl Beech, Edge Ministries, CVM

'There are not many books on discipleship written from experience and an in-depth knowledge. In this book, Rev Henry takes us through to a deeper understanding of our relationship with Jesus who is the image of our invisible God.

'*The Transformed Follower* brings the reader closer to a very deep knowledge and understanding of Jesus Christ as we travel through the journey of life. "There are many roads we travel on in our lives and many opportunities for Him to draw alongside us so we may encounter His presence."

'I will recommend this book to everyone who desires to have an in-depth knowledge of Christ the Messiah.'
Felix Adepoju, Senior Pastor and founder of Christ Light International Christian Centre, Rainham and Clacton-on-Sea

'If you want to know about the call of God on your life, the authority that He's given us and our mission as followers (disciples) of Christ, then I strongly suggest you read this book and be prepared to be challenged and changed. As followers of Christ, as we allow Him to transform us, so we are empowered and released to transform our communities.

'This book gives many challenges that we as comfortable disciples need to hear and act upon. It encourages us to assess our own lives and be less self-centred and more outwardly focused to a lost and hurting community. It is a book that encourages intimacy with Christ which in turn motivates disciples into service for Him.

'Why do we exist?

'What is our purpose in this world?

'If these are some of your questions, please read this book and be prepared for God to transform you from the inside out.'
Rev Andrew Knight, Elim Church Braintree

'A very personal and powerful testimony runs throughout this book, combining experienced life events and manifestations of the Holy Spirit with the outworking of Scripture through Henry's life. There is a deep message of transformation for individuals but also for the Church; the book shares what one might experience when they are saved and how that could be lived out corporately. This beautiful description of the transformed Church living in the transformed Love of Christ helped validate my own discernments and feelings.'
Captain Richard Wearmouth, Salvation Army Officer

'Discipleship is a major and key value running throughout Christianity. The Gospels record Jesus beginning His earthly ministry by calling His disciples, and among His final words of instruction to those disciples was that they "make disciples of all nations".

'In this book, Henry Pradella sets out a great biblical basis and praxis to enable Jesus' disciples to carry on His ministry to make disciples of all nations. Definitely worth a read.'
David Campbell, Member of the National Leadership Team of the Elim Pentecostal Church.

'A challenging and thought-provoking read. Henry tackles various aspects of our walk with Christ, showing how God uses His Word to lay a foundation to bring transformation and empowerment to a believer's life. May God use this book to probe your heart and bring a greater change in your life through His truth.'
Michael Ovenden, Outreach Coordinator, Teen Challenge London

The Transformed Follower

Where Ordinary and Extraordinary Embrace

Henry Pradella

instant apostle

First published in Great Britain in 2023

Instant Apostle
104A The Drive
Rickmansworth
Herts
WD3 4DU

Copyright © Henry Pradella 2023

The author has asserted his rights under Section 77 of the Copyright, Designs and Patents Act, 1988, to be identified as the author of the work.

All rights reserved. No portion of this book may be reproduced or transmitted in any form or by any means, electronic or mechanical, including photocopying and recording, or by any information storage and retrieval system, without permission in writing from the publisher.

Unless otherwise indicated, all Scripture quotations are taken from the New King James Version®. Copyright © 1982 by Thomas Nelson. Used by permission. All rights reserved.

Scripture quotations marked 'NCV' are taken from the New Century Version®. Copyright © 2005 by Thomas Nelson. Used by permission. All rights reserved.

Scripture quotations marked 'NIV' are taken from the Holy Bible, New International Version® Anglicised, NIV® Copyright © 1979, 1984, 2011 by Biblica, Inc.® Used by permission. All rights reserved worldwide.

Every effort has been made to seek permission to use copyright material reproduced in this book. The publisher apologises for those cases where permission might not have been sought and, if notified, will formally seek permission at the earliest opportunity.

The views and opinions expressed in this work are those of the author and do not necessarily reflect the views and opinions of the publisher.

British Library Cataloguing-in-Publication Data

A catalogue record for this book is available from the British Library.

This book and all other Instant Apostle books are available from Instant Apostle:

Website: www.instantapostle.com

Email: info@instantapostle.com

ISBN 978-1-912726-77-6

Printed in Great Britain.

To
Our precious children, Paul and Sarah,
our daughter-in-law Louise
and our son-in-law Nicolas.
Chosen, Called and Loved

Acknowledgements

This book could not have been written without the support and encouragement of so many different people. But first and foremost, I want to emphasise the significant vision, passion and insight given by the Holy Spirit's guidance and prompting in making this second book possible. It is His divine inspiration that has consistently driven this writing with the conviction and insight that made it possible.

Thank you, Sheryl, for believing in and supporting me again in this work and walking with me every step of the way in its creation; your encouragement, practical suggestions, reminders and tweaks have helped clarify my thinking and direction.

Again, I want to thank the team at Instant Apostle for their encouragement, trust and invitation to bring this publication about. To Nicki, Sheila, Nigel and Anne for your professional advice and guidance in every part of this process from editing to final print. Thank you for giving me the opportunity again to make this project a reality.

Also, my thanks to those of you who have endorsed this book amid your busy schedules, and for the good wishes I have received from you and others who have backed this project.

Finally, I want to thank the wonderful fellowship Sheryl and I have been welcomed into at Elim Church. You are an amazing family of brothers and sisters in Christ and an inspiration to us. It is so exciting to see all that God is doing in our midst as we journey together with Him, seeing the wonderful seedbed He is unfolding, cultivating, and releasing of His kingdom purposes for this community.

Contents

Prologue 13
Introduction 17
Part 1: The Call of Following 25
    1: Catching Our Attention 27
    2: By Him, Through Him, with Him 47
    3: Following with Intent 62
    4: Essential Grace 74
    5: Staying Focused 86
Part 2: The Nature of Following 107
    6: Capacity to Grow 109
    7: Positioned for Purpose 121
    8: Maintaining Identity 135
    9: Faith Walks on Water 145
    10: The Fusion of Diversity 159
Part 3: The Expectations of Following 173
    11: The Attitude of Being 175
    12: Foundational Hallmarks 186
    13: Yearning for More 204
    14: The Lamp of Purity and Peace 218
    15: Conflicts and Challenges 230
    16: Heartfelt Treasure 245

Prologue

This is a book about discipleship, born out of my experience, understanding and journey with the God who called me to follow Him. At its heart is a relationship with Jesus; a journey of discovery, of challenge and of change, because by its very nature when we choose to follow Him it requires movement. It involves transformation. It is about trust.

But what does that mean? When we look at the Gospel accounts in Scripture, we discover there were many who admired Jesus, seeing Him as a prophet, a great teacher, a miracle worker or a healer. Some looked to Him as the Messiah; the Christ sent from God.[1]

There were those who came looking for guidance, healing or personal gain through selfish ambitions and agendas and, once received (or not), left.[2] There were those who hung around on the fringe, caught up in His popularity like fans of a celebrity, but remained on the outside.[3]

There were others, like some of the religious leaders, who followed to keep an eye on Him and scrutinise His every word; to see if He was doing or saying things that would rock their orthodox religious boat, so to speak. At times they attempted to bait Him with controversial questions to catch Him out, but failed.[4]

---

[1] Matthew 7:28-29; 8:16; Luke 9:18-19; 23:8; John 1:41.
[2] Luke 10:25-29; Luke 17:11-19; Luke 18:18-23.
[3] Matthew 4:23-25; Matthew 13:1-2; Matthew 15:29-31.
[4] Matthew 12:9-14; 19:3-9; Luke 20:20-26; John 8:3-9;

And then there were those whom He called with two simple words, 'Follow Me.'[5] And they did. He still calls people today to follow Him.

But what kind of a follower might you be? Would you call yourself a disciple of Jesus at all? And if so, how would you define the nature of your discipleship? Would others recognise that you follow Jesus? Would they look at you and say, 'I can see you follow Jesus because you stand out a mile'? Or is your discipleship invisible?

The nature of following someone or something has many sides to it. I can follow someone at a distance and remain unseen, whereby the influence of the one I am following is so slight it has little impact on my life and, as such, changes nothing. I am, in that sense, following as a spectator, merely an onlooker, an observer with curiosity. I may choose to identify with other followers, but only in so far as it does not cost me anything or demand any devotion or commitment on my time or lifestyle.

When we say to Jesus, 'Yes, I will follow You,' what are we signing up to? How far are we prepared to go as His disciple? Where do we personally draw the line? Jesus headed for a bloody death on a barbaric Roman cross. Are we prepared to go there?

Is our perspective and understanding of following Him the same as that of Jesus, or are they different? At what point would we say, as some of His disciples did, that this is too hard for us to contemplate continuing, and turn away?[6]

These are some hard-hitting questions I am inviting us to consider. My hope is that this book encourages each of us with some signposts to help us process for ourselves what this journey with and into Christ is about and what it might involve. It is designed to equip our thinking and response, as well as being an opportunity to reflect on what Jesus intended when calling followers, what He taught us about discipleship and what

---

[5] Matthew 4:18-22; Luke 5:27-28; John 1:43.
[6] John 6:60,66.

that might look like for us today in the communities He has called us to be a part of.

Introduction

We live in a consumerist society. We buy into a lifestyle that focuses on a worldly perspective, whereby the improvement of the material self is promoted and encouraged. Our self-image is deemed as all-important in such an environment and we are constantly under pressure to improve our appearance, our status, our home comforts, our wealth and possessions and our reputation.

To a greater or lesser degree, it is an inherent part of our human nature. We want the best for ourselves and our loved ones, and in some cases we will go to great lengths to achieve our goals and aims in a manner we perceive as justifiable to create and live a comfortable and safe lifestyle.

Most of us do not go looking for God; not consciously, anyway. But Jesus came looking for us; for you and me. He once said to His disciples, 'You did not choose Me, but I chose you' (John 15:16). A relationship with God was the last thing I was looking for, but when I encountered Him in Jesus, it changed everything.

Following Jesus is transformational. You cannot follow Him and remain unchanged or unmoved. He will turn the experience of your life upside down – and, I need to add, for the better. He will bring you into a fullness and richness of life like nothing else can. There is no passivity when we choose to go with Him where He goes. As such, we are called to discipleship, not consumerism.

Before returning to His Father, Jesus left His followers with a commission. It was specific: to go out into all the nations of the world and 'make disciples' (Matthew 28:18-20). It was noticeably clearcut.

Jesus put this assignment into a particular context. After His death and resurrection, all authority had been placed back in His hands. Everything that is both seen and unseen in the physical and spiritual realms is subject to His sovereign reign. There are no exceptions, no exemptions. He reigns over all things and all things are subject to Him.

He commissioned His disciples from that place of complete authority. It means when He sends us out to 'make disciples', we go in that authority and, as such, carry the full weight of who He is and what He represents. Because His authority extends over all things and all places, we are called and sent to all nations; to every place and every people group on the earth, and continue to be until He returns.

Jesus did not say, make disciples '*in* all the nations', but '*of* all the nations' (Matthew 28:19, my italics). The expectation is that there are no areas where His reign cannot reach; no nations or people groups that are exempt. We are to assume that such an assignment is not only achievable, but the requirement by which we are sent.

We rightly rejoice when we see people come to faith in Jesus and see new members become part of our church fellowship and family. But we must not be complacent in thinking we are successful when there remain so many in our communities who are still outside that right relationship with God.

We can be obsessed with church figures, while God is looking at the population of nations, not churches. We continue to be a people sent into a world of need, to places spiritually dying and lost, without hope or meaning, however glossy the surface looks.

Jesus also emphasised what making disciples involves. There are three things that He instructs us to do: to make, to baptise and to teach. We cannot simply expect people to come to church based on programme-driven initiatives and invitations alone. Enabling people to come to faith, equipping them to grow in that faith and releasing them to share that faith is a process and not just a decision. It is not something we sign up to, but a journey we undertake; a journey that is relational, not religious.

Whatever the means of our mission, primarily we are sharing the good news of Jesus Christ, enabling others to come to an informed understanding and experience of such love as is available and accessible.

> How then shall they call on Him in whom they have not believed? And how shall they believe in Him of whom they have not heard? And how shall they hear without a preacher? And how shall they preach unless they are sent? As it is written:
> 'How beautiful are the feet of those who preach the gospel of peace,
> Who bring glad tidings of good things!'
> *Romans 10:14-15*

There are many ways God leads us into His presence, but we must acknowledge that it is His Holy Spirit who convicts us. By ourselves, we can convert no one to faith in Jesus. And yet He commissioned us to be the means by which others discover His grace and mercy, poured out in love for them, when He told us to 'go' out there into every place. That must mean stepping out and engaging with the world, where we are called to love and to serve with the same compassion and effectiveness that Jesus had when He went around the various communities He engaged with.

It was there that people witnessed the love of God displayed with a compassionate heart that clearly and practically demonstrated the fact that people matter to Him, and He loves each one of us passionately. It was there principally that Jesus trained and released those disciples He initially gathered to follow Him, sending them to do everything He did. Everything!

This was what drew people to Him. He was followed

everywhere by droves of people wanting to see Him and engage with Him. He made people feel important and valued. He cared for them like no one had before. He met people's needs, bringing them hope and direction. He pointed them to a loving Father. And people responded. People will always respond to the practical nature of servanthood that demonstrates compassion. People wanted to follow Him. And many did.

We are not only precious and valued, but we all have an assignment to make Him known and extend His kingdom further. He has called disciples to make disciples, who in turn are to make disciples, who themselves then go out and make more disciples, and so on.

For us to grow into the stature and confidence of our calling, we need to be taught and equipped to be fully operational and mature to carry the weight of His presence, authority and power in us. This is not merely a passing on of information or doctrine or belief.

Jesus sent His disciples out, trained, equipped and authorised, that they might influence and transform the communities to which He directed them.[7] Not only that, but He also promised that He would be with them 'always'.[8]

I believe one of the significant challenges we have as the Church is to evaluate how effectively we disciple people to grow in maturity and fully discover their place and gifting as followers of Christ. It is here, in the intimacy of a relationship with God, empowered by the Holy Spirit, that we grow and walk in our unique calling, released in all that equips us to engage in the mission of God in extending His kingdom everywhere.

I wonder if, over the centuries, we have too often bought into a consumerist approach, whereby we have become too dependent on the 'leader at the front' to feed us, pray for us, pastor us, advise us and encourage us. Is that perhaps why there are some in our churches who struggle with the call to mission in sharing their lives openly in their community, witnessing to

---

[7] Matthew 10:5-8; Luke 10:1,9.
[8] Matthew 28:20.

the love of Christ while demonstrating the authority He has given us with the power to change the lives of others?

A consumerist dependency on our pastors and leaders can weaken our foundation and leave us powerless and lacking in confidence as to who we are in Christ. It can create an anxiety, fear or hesitation when it comes to sharing our faith with others to draw them to Jesus. It can stifle a passionate boldness to step into the darkness of a needy world with a light that burns inside, bursting to be released.

I do not believe it was ever Jesus' intention for His disciples to be feeble and weak in this commission. He calls us each into a relationship with Him that is transformational and empowering, bringing us life in 'all its fullness' (John 10:10, NCV).

Yes, there needs to be a structural hierarchy in the body to envision, motivate and equip, but also to release us in mission, in the context of a functioning organism and influential powerhouse that gathers others through its servanthood and love.

The apostle Paul puts it like this:

> And He Himself gave some *to be* apostles, some prophets, some evangelists, and some pastors and teachers, for the equipping of the saints for the work of ministry, for the edifying of the body of Christ, till we all come to the unity of the faith and of the knowledge of the Son of God, to a perfect man, to the measure of the stature of the fullness of Christ.
> *Ephesians 4:11-13*

Notice some of the phraseology here; for equipping and edifying into the measure and stature of the fullness of Christ; to be fully like Him. But who is that? The saints. That is all of us. That is what our discipleship must embrace; equipping and releasing us into ministry through all the different means by which each one of us has been called.

When we become reluctant to step into this transformational

empowerment, we not only deprive ourselves of the possibilities that might follow, but we also inhibit the mission of the whole body of the Church and as a result prevent those outside from discovering fully the salvation that is available to them, for which Jesus paid such a heavy price.

I do not know if it has always been the case where commitment to our calling is viewed by some with an element of uncertainty, indifference, apathy, lack of understanding of our purpose, or not perceiving it as significantly as God does. We certainly read about an emboldened early Church in the book of Acts, who stepped out with courage and conviction that saw many, almost daily, come into a right relationship with Jesus; and the Church just grew and grew.[9]

Perhaps we feel we do not have that kind of impact, influence or authority any more to change the environment and community around us. Some might consider we live in a world and time of advancement and sophistication, where such faith and impetus are no longer relevant or important. Some might even conclude that faith in God is history and His Church insignificant in our modern age.

Certainly, the enemy would want to feed us with that lie; that we are powerless and insignificant, and in so doing intimidate us with all kinds of excuses to not engage in this mission to which we were born. If that is the case, then he will have succeeded. But I want to remind you that God is greater than that, and it is He who calls us to walk with Him and to step into all the potential that He wants to release through us. You and I are an essential part in this story of His ongoing mission.

Perhaps part of our reluctance may be about our identity, or more specifically, lack of; in not fully knowing who we are and what we have been called to. That is certainly the nature of consumerism. We depend on external sources to create an outward identity that at its core is fragile and temperamental; a 'feed-me' culture that leaves us lacking in the essential nature of

---

[9] Acts 2:40-47.

being deeply rooted in and centred on Jesus; being like Him.

God came Himself to seek you and me out; to draw us to Himself through His reconciling and sacrificial love; to empower us in that love and to send us out to witness and demonstrate it to others. That is what it means to be called; to embrace a journey that transforms us, grows us and releases us into a broken world.

Part 1

The Call of Following

1

Catching Our Attention

What does following involve? What does it commit us to? And most importantly, who exactly is it we are called to follow? Jesus did not say, 'Come and find me.' He said, 'Come and follow me.' There is a world of difference between looking for someone and being found by that person.

Throughout our lives we are all influenced by people in one way or another, and at the same time we influence others, be it our families, our friends, our work colleagues, church members and all the other relational contacts we have. We are continually subjected to a myriad of different inputs from both within and outside our framework of relationships; the likes of advertising, social media, political ideologies, superstars and celebrities we rightly or wrongly look up to, influential speakers and leaders, whether religious or political. The list is endless.

All of these, to one degree or another, affect our everyday lives. Some of these influences are seasonal, whereby we go through phases of buying into a particular idea, belief or viewpoint because it suits our circumstances at the time, or we may need that input in the issues we are experiencing at that moment. At other times, influences can be lifelong or life-changing.

If we are honest, when someone unfamiliar says to us, 'Come with me,' or, 'Follow me,' most of us try to weigh up the options. We want to know first who they are and what their motives might be in beckoning us. We want to know where we are going. We want to assure ourselves that we are not being conned or putting ourselves in any kind of danger or disadvantage by accepting such a vague invitation.

Of course, there are times when we can be naïve and gullible and easily lured into something we later regret, just because of a whim or momentary lapse of thinking. As such, we walk into it with our eyes shut.

When Jesus approached individuals such as fishermen, tax collectors, zealots and the like and beckoned them to follow Him, with the vaguest of promises such as, 'Follow me, and I will make you fishers of men' (Matthew 4:19), I wonder what would have been going through their minds to drop everything so readily and go after Him?

Yes, Jesus' reputation was beginning to get around through word of mouth and they would have already been exposed to Him in a limited way before He called them. Yet something inside persuaded them they were doing the right thing because there was little hesitation that we know of in their response. They just got up and followed. Challenged or curious, they went with Him.

Andrew and another began as disciples of John the Baptist.[10] People were listening to this prophet's proclamation and call to repentance, and many were baptised in the process. He always pointed people away from himself and towards Jesus.[11] John did not beat about the bush with the urgency of his preaching. When the time was right, it was clear to him that his two followers now needed to 'switch tracks' and so pointed them to Jesus with a declaration that caught their attention: 'And looking at Jesus as He walked, he said, "Behold the Lamb of God!"' (John 1:36). It was the second time in two days John used this term concerning Jesus.[12]

I suppose at various times in our lives, we make decisions

---

[10] John 1:35-42.
[11] John 1:25-27
[12] John 1:29.

concerning our lifestyles and who we socially associate with. Sometimes we divert our allegiances and pursue new directions through invitation, conviction or opportunity. Whether career changes, new relationships or friendship groups, our social networks can change, expand or divert.

Now here is an interesting thought. How would you introduce Jesus to someone you hope would come to know and follow Him? John did not simply say, 'Look guys, that's the One I've been talking about,' or, 'This is the one you need to tag onto from now on.' Instead, John identified Jesus prophetically by the most important aspect of who He was in terms of what He came to accomplish. 'Behold, the Lamb of God!' Jesus was made known by the sacrifice He came to endure and suffer for our sake, perhaps in reference to the Suffering Servant prophecy of Isaiah 53.

Was it this that captivated the inquisitiveness of these two disciples, as they then chased after Jesus? They certainly caught His attention when He stopped, turned around and asked them what they wanted. They responded with a bland opening question, as you do when you want to engage someone in conversation; like, 'Hi, not seen you around here before,' or, 'What do you do?' or, as in this case, 'Where are You staying?' (John 1:38). And the offer was taken up with, 'Come and see' (John 1:39).

The invitation, I would suggest, was to follow Him. Perhaps that was the pull they needed; just a 'come and see'. We are invited to be where He is. I do not think these two disciples knew at that stage where that was going to lead them.

How might that pan out in our relationship with Jesus, where trust is required, when we are not given a map or schedule? It should bring several questions to mind if we are serious. How committed are we in following? What are our expectations of Jesus? Who or what do we anticipate engaging with? What might we hope to discover? Where might that take us?

Jesus doesn't take us into the unknown, but into His known. He knows where He is going and where He wants us to be. But it requires surrender and commitment on our part. He is constantly on the move and takes us with Him. It is a journey that can take us out of our comfortable and familiar setting. It needs to become our priority if we are to truly fulfil His purpose for us.

When I was nine years old and for the first time, as a family, we went to visit my relatives in Poland, we stopped off en route at my uncle and aunt's apartment in Germany and stayed with them a couple of days. It was a particularly significant time for my mother and father, who had not seen any of their relatives since leaving Poland at the start of the Second World War.

There was much excitement all round and an emotional coming together after so many years apart. Not having children of their own, my uncle and aunt intended to spoil us somewhat by taking us on an expensive shopping spree. My treat was a train set and my sister's an 'all-singing, all-dancing' doll, which she adored.

When we got back to their apartment, my father and uncle proceeded to unpack the train set and put it together. They then started to play with it. I'm not sure I got a look in. They were like two little children at Christmas. Their excuse, when I tried to muscle in, was that they were just checking to make sure it worked properly. I'm sure many parents use that line when playing with their children's toys.

Where am I going with this? It's about branching out. The tracks of this train set made up a basic oval shape and so the locomotive and two attached carriages just went round and round with the occasional variation of going the other way, or the loco pushing rather than pulling. But that's all it did.

I wonder if at times we can get stuck in a rut in our churches in a similar way, where things can just go round and round in a predictable fashion year after year, with the occasional alteration. We can become so conditioned to the familiar that our expectations remain static and our anticipation of something else, something different, remains diminished. I'm not sure that is what God intends His church to be like. Do you? If not, then what?

Following that first visit to Germany, my uncle began to send me additional parts for the train set, beginning with a pair of turnout tracks where I could switch and branch out onto another section, another line and direction. It opened up all kinds of possibilities and diverse layouts, as you can imagine. Gone was the familiar repetition and in came explorative ventures. More tracks and more trains were added year upon year. The whole thing grew. And when I outgrew it, the whole investment was passed on to my son and he in turn passed it on to his son.

Isn't that what following Jesus is about? To switch tracks and branch out into ever new ventures of encounter and engagement, where He takes us to new places, new opportunities and ever-expanding kingdom dynamics that we can embrace and pass on to others.

For Andrew and the other disciple, it was an intriguing start. Jesus showed them where He was staying, and they remained with Him the rest of that day. That was not the end, but the beginning. They would no doubt have spent time talking, asking questions, listening with intrigue to all Jesus shared with them; and, I suggest, wanting more.

I wonder if at times we appreciate just who He is, in the fullness of His splendour and majesty and awe; the One who came to redeem humankind from the tyranny of sin that caused wrecked lives and subjected the whole of creation to be corrupted and off kilter. I wonder if we recognise the immense privilege it is to be in His presence; He who is above all things, greater than all things, who holds all things, who restores all things. I would imagine if we could truly and fully comprehend Him, we would not want to leave His side. What could possibly be more captivating than an invitation to be with Him? Committing ongoing time in His presence, putting everything else aside and just being with Him and seeing what He shows us, tells us, releases to us and where He directs our path. That is precious time.

When Jesus beckoned them both to 'come and see', He was not showing them His headquarters or a head office of His mission. Where He was staying was not a permanent residency. Jesus would have no 'fixed abode' in this mission. There is no consumerism involved here; no supporters club to sign up to. Just a journey that requires sacrifice and perhaps even hardship, because our anchor and foundation are not in a building or an institution, but a person, who is constantly on the move and takes us with Him.

And so came others too, one after another that He gathered, as the team grew. A team of followers heading who knows where. For the next three years they went wherever Jesus went. They journeyed together, ate together; did everything together. And in that time, they saw extraordinary things. They were taken way out of their comfort zones and way beyond any earthly experience they could possibly imagine. It was at times so far-fetched it was blowing their minds, yet at the same time, quite ordinary in the context of where they found themselves travelling. But still they followed and witnessed and experienced and joined in and did as He did. They were being transformed in the process; shaped to be all they were created and called to be.

These obscure, unknown individuals would in time turn the world upside down. Mike Breen writes:

> It doesn't appear that Jesus chooses these guys on the basis of their resumes or their spiritual gift inventories. He simply offers them a relationship with himself and a vision to follow.[13]

We are first called into relationship with Jesus. In the outworking of that relationship, an equipping and commissioning is released, for walking in His purposes. It is here we begin to discover the uniqueness of who we are and

---

[13] Mike Breen and Walt Kallestad, *The Passionate Church* (Eastbourne: Kingsway, 2005), p112.

what we are called to.

But why? What was it all for? Jesus did not come to start another religion, but to reconcile the world to God by restoring a broken relationship with Him. He did this by demonstrating God's love for humanity through His teaching and healing miracles, and through signs and wonders; but also, and ultimately, to sacrifice His life on a cross, thus destroying and removing the barrier between humanity and God that sin created.

It is significant to understand that Jesus accomplished this as a man, with human limitations but empowered by God's Holy Spirit. As such, He modelled what He wanted us to embrace and live under. He brings His world into ours and wants us to continue to live under His kingdom reign and draw others into it.

Stepping into the unexpected

So how does following begin for us? For some, encountering and coming to know God in a personal way can be sudden, unexpected and dramatic. For others, it can be a more gentle and gradual process of discovery. God knows and understands each one of us personally, even before we know Him. As such, He knows the kind of approach to make, for us to engage with and accept the offer He presents us with to follow Him.

Our character, personality and experience of life shape and influence how we respond. As such, God is mindful that encountering Him as a loving Father, who has our best interests at heart and longs to draw us close to Him, needs to be experienced in a way that will not cause us to be fearful and run away.

Some of us need a gentle approach to come to terms with and process such an invitation, whereby coming to faith is a steady and measured unfolding. It is a journey that encourages a fragile or tentative mindset that may be cautious, sceptical or uncertain of the truth that God by His Holy Spirit presents us with, to settle in our hearts over time.

For others, our lifestyle may need a radical or dramatic change of direction, and the only way God can draw our attention to Himself is through a sudden sharp shock of an encounter, where we do not have the space or time to rationalise or dismiss His offer, because He knows, left to our own devices, we would not respond in a positive way. That was certainly the case in my experience. Having grown up in a strict but loving Christian family and steeped in biblical and doctrinal teaching, you could argue I had all the resources necessary to maintain and grow in faith, and on one level that was true. But as a young and impressionable teenager with the world in front of me and presented with all kinds of exciting and seductive experiences and world views, an external religious diet did not touch the place in me that longed to discover something more, and it soon led me to turn away from the Church and, consequently, to turn away from God.

My previous participation through a religious lens rather than a relational place of belonging was the only way I knew how to experience God. In this indifferent and rebellious lifestyle a divine encounter took place; when I least expected it and, to be honest, was not in the least bit looking for it.

Why this dramatic way? Because God knew it would be the only means by which He would get my full attention. In that, His timing was everything and, in fact, crucial for things to come to a head, where surrender to His call was not only possible in my self-centred lifestyle but had become desirable. In my previous book, *I AM Relational*, I describe that encounter with Jesus, which transformed my experience of God from an external religious observance to a relational reality and the dramatic impact it had on my life. It was an experience from which there was no looking back or returning to what I had previously known:

> In the core of my being I came face to face with Jesus, not visible to my eyes, but visible to my soul. Everything that I had grown up with and was taught about God

suddenly made sense, but not just in my head. This was encounter that reached right into my heart. It was relational. It was a 'knowing' that no mere explanation could describe. It was a reality that left me sitting there for a while, unable to move or to stand. I felt physically drained, as if I'd just run a marathon. Something had shifted. An awakening that relocated my perspective about who I was… and who He was.[14]

It was, I imagine, a similar case for the apostle Paul, who was undoubtedly more extreme in His hostility towards a young and growing Church movement he was vehemently opposed to. I would not have described my rejection of the Church as hostile, just indifferent.

Paul, or Saul as he was then known, was a staunch Pharisee, zealous for his Jewish tradition, steeped in the Old Testament and defending its orthodoxy as he perceived it, for its identity and integrity to be maintained and upheld. He viewed this radical new movement of Christian disciples growing and spreading before him as a threat to his ordered religious way of life. So much so, he obtained official documents from the religious authorities to hunt down, arrest, imprison and, if necessary, kill any he came across, to halt the spread of this perceived threat.

Paul was focused, headstrong and determined in his mission. Nothing would deter him from his conviction, until the day he set out from Jerusalem on his way to Damascus, to round up culprits there:

> Then Saul, still breathing threats and murder against the disciples of the Lord, went to the high priest and asked letters from him to the synagogues of Damascus, so that if he found any who were of the Way, whether men or women, he might bring them bound to Jerusalem.
> *Acts 9:1-2*

---

[14] Henry Pradella, *I AM Relational* (Watford: Instant Apostle, 2020), p85.

Sometimes we can be blinded to the circumstances we surround ourselves with, while pursuing an agenda filled with hatred or rage, where our equilibrium appears threatened or displaced. It can make us irrational in our thinking and give us a warped perspective because our way of life can feel endangered or challenged by circumstances or people outside our control. We can become preoccupied with hostility, prejudice and vendetta against what we perceive as an intrusion into our familiar and ordered world view.

As Paul journeyed to Damascus with fellow men alongside him, the day would no doubt have been firmly formulated in his mind. His game plan played out in his thoughts of the scenario upon arriving in Damascus; the fulfilment of this mission, and the added satisfaction and expectation of travelling back to Jerusalem leading an entourage of captive disciples of Jesus.

The day, however, was about to turn out in a way very different from what Paul had envisaged. It was in every sense a divine ambush. Heavenly light pierced him and threw him to the ground. A voice then confronted and questioned him concerning the motives for his persecution. Paul, by now startled, trembling and in shock at this sudden and unexpected encounter, tried to comprehend what was happening, questioning who he was hearing and what was going on; as would we all, in such a situation.

> And he said, 'Who are You, Lord?'
> Then the Lord said, 'I am Jesus, whom you are persecuting. It *is* hard for you to kick against the goads.'
> *Acts 9:5*

Jesus gives an intriguing response here. Paul is not accused of persecuting the Church, but of persecuting Jesus Himself. This is an important and significant point. Any persecution directed at a disciple of Jesus is an assault on Jesus Himself. Why? Because they are one. There is a bond of unity between Jesus and His church as one body. It is relational and it is intimate.

A follower of Jesus is therefore not someone who tags on at

a distance behind, nor even someone who walks alongside, but someone who is indwelt by the very presence of God in Jesus Christ. It is that close, that intimate. It puts our relationship with God into quite a personal context. Even in our struggles and difficulties in life, He is there in the midst of it all.

It is fascinating how within such a scenario as Paul's encounter on this road, one person can be touched in a life-changing way while others around are hardly affected. 'And the men who journeyed with him stood speechless, hearing a voice but seeing no one' (Acts 9:7). It is a mystery how God can act in a crowd of people whereby some encounter His presence and others barely know anything has happened. I suggest that has partly to do with calling.

It was Paul, and not his companions, who was called directly by Jesus, not merely for the sake of being warned off from his persecuting agenda, but because God had a greater purpose for his life; a life Paul would not only be drawn into, but one in which he would also suffer hardship and danger, for the sake of accomplishing all that God had ordained for him. In the end it would cost him his life.

His shift in missional direction would lead him to champion the very people he was so determined to destroy. He was equipped for such a calling because all his previous life experiences and zeal for God would now be channelled into expanding rather than demolishing the very Church he had been chasing after. He would experience the *agape* love that was at the centre of this fledgling Christian fellowship. All his energies would now be put into strengthening, equipping, teaching, planting and expanding this Church for the sake of extending the kingdom of God and making Jesus known further and further afield.

When God calls us into that relationship of following Him, it is not a random choice He makes. Nor is it, for example, like that of an employer, appointing someone in the context of hiring or recruiting them for a task or job; having advertised the post, asked for applications, interviewed candidates and then selected the most appropriate interviewee from a short list, based on their character, experience and qualifications. Jesus did not and does not use any such criteria. Calling us is deliberate and specific. You and I were called long before any of us were created. It was not based on anything we have done or could do that would merit His choosing us. Nor is His calling dependent on our condition or status, but on His purpose and will for us. Paul describes it like this:

> And we know that all things work together for good to those who love God, to those who are the called according to *His* purpose. For whom He foreknew, He also predestined *to be* conformed to the image of His Son, that He might be the firstborn among many brethren. Moreover whom He predestined, these He also called; whom He called, these He also justified; and whom He justified, these He also glorified.
> *Romans 8:28-30*

While this is not initiated by us but by Him, what each of us is called to cannot be accomplished by anyone else in the way we would accomplish it. You and I are that unique and precious in our individuality. We are that significant; called to a purpose uniquely our own. We each have an individual and collective relationship with Him and, as such, form part of His body.[15]

We have free will, certainly. God is not dictatorial. But even if I choose to reject that which I have been called to and it is given to another, it will be implemented differently because my uniqueness is different from theirs. It is in and through what I bring to the task that my calling is significant and why I have been purposed for it. That applies to each one of us.

He knows our strengths and weaknesses and encourages us not only to follow Him but, in the process, in our daily walk, also to be transformed by Him. Our identity lies in Him as part of His body, yet is uniquely individual in it, as different as an eye

---

[15] 1 Corinthians 12:27.

is to an ear or a foot to a hand.[16] Whether that calling is gradual or sudden, I believe God was already at work in us long before we became conscious of it.

Did you notice something else Jesus confronted Paul with, in that encounter on the journey to Damascus? He highlighted Paul's wrestling with himself and struggling with something that lay inside, whereby he was 'kick[ing] against the goads' (Acts 9:5). What did Jesus mean? What was He referring to? A goad was a tool used by herdsmen for driving or spurring on cattle and other livestock, to guide their movement and direction. It was like a spiked stick used for prodding if the animal became stubborn.

What was Paul fighting against or resistant to? Because clearly there was something going on inside him which Jesus recognised and identified when He made that comment to him. It seems Paul was so obsessed with this movement and any alternative form of religious viewpoint or ideology to that of the Jewish faith he knew and cherished that he found himself fighting unknowingly with God Himself.

Paul may have been resolute and steadfast in his determination to stamp out this Christian Church, but I would suggest maybe there was something else niggling him inside that was unsettling; something that perhaps made him feel uneasy with some of his actions, however justified he convinced himself he was in carrying out his persecutions.

As a Pharisee and prominent figure in the religious council, he would have been committed to serving God in the Jewish faith that he had been brought up in, and the service he had been trained for under the guidance of his teacher, Gamaliel.[17] Perhaps something of God would have been stirring in him and making him become increasingly uncomfortable with what he saw in himself. There may have been doubts in his mind over some of the teaching of this 'sect', as he saw it, that he would have heard about, and some of that may have started to filter

---

[16] 1 Corinthians 12:14-16.
[17] Acts 22:3.

into his heart. 'What if they are right?' It's an interesting thought.

I certainly remember the years I had drifted away from the Church and any connection with God as a time that occasionally made me feel unsettled and uncomfortable when any mention or conversation about religion came up. I could not tell you specifically what it was, but the fact that something was gnawing away at me amid my 'secular' lifestyle was at times creating an awkward longing for, and yet at the same time rejection of, an undiscovered truth inside that was subconsciously there, waiting to burst out, even though I would not then have said I recognised it for what it was.

God can often be drawing us closer by first making us feel uncomfortable with our lifestyle, or our actions, or even our attitudes, whether towards ourselves or others. There then comes a growing restlessness with our 'lot'. It is here that an inner challenge starts to grow; a seed planted that begins to germinate and preoccupy us, even if subconsciously, creating not so much doubt as longing.

This is certainly what I experienced long before surrendering my life to God. It is a longing for something we feel is missing or not quite whole in our lives. It is a gap in our inner being that only God can fill; a hunger that only He can satisfy. 'And Jesus said to them, "I am the bread of life. He who comes to Me shall never hunger, and he who believes in Me shall never thirst"' (John 6:35).

Sometimes it causes us to ask questions of ourselves as dissatisfaction spreads and we become more open to possibilities; the possibility that God may be speaking to us. Perhaps that prodding by God is something we all experience in one way or another when we have strayed away and are distant from Him. Whether as a sprint or as a marathon, we then begin to engage with that wrestling inside until we answer the call from the place of 'knowing' deep down, whether strongly or tentatively, that beckons us... 'Follow Me.'

Immobilised to be mobilised

I expect many of us have experienced situations that have seemed bizarre, even nightmarish, where our whole world suddenly hits the buffers because of something unexpected that has emerged. It feels surreal and leaves us in a daze and our normal rational perception abandons us. We go through all the worst-case scenarios, hoping we will suddenly wake up and it will all have been just a bad dream.

Paul, temporarily blinded by his encounter on the road, was led by his companions into Damascus. For three days he remained there without sight, neither eating nor drinking.[18] The whole episode would no doubt have been replaying in his mind, over and over, as he wrestled with trying to make sense of it all.

As Paul prayed, he may well have been fearful that his sight would not return; thinking the unthinkable, that this staunch and influential figure would now be reduced to begging on the streets. His ego totally shattered and deflated. His world had suddenly and unexpectedly fallen apart and there seemed no respite, no apparent let-up… for three days.

Sometimes God needs to immobilise us to mobilise us. We can often live such busy and hurried lives that we miss opportunities to slow down or stop and reflect on our life's journey and the direction we are heading in. The familiar routine, however pressurised, can sometimes seem more acceptable than an unknown stepping out into something new and different. We are often creatures of habit. We make assumptions about how our life is likely to pan out. Sometimes God requires our whole undivided attention to really speak to us. Sometimes we need to be 'sidelined' for that to happen.

Following my encounter with Jesus in that powerful and profound way, I had imagined my life would continue in the way I had planned; that somehow this new-found relationship with God would weave into my lifestyle, my ambitions and

---

[18] Acts 9:8-9.

aspirations, and the direction I chose for myself. I had anticipated remaining in teaching, with perhaps some form of church attachment and involvement tagged on.

But the journey He was taking me (and my wife, Sheryl) on was anything but. The problem was, I was not listening, even though He was shouting loud and clear. I loved my teaching role. I loved the students, the staff I worked alongside, the subject I taught, the pastoral work I was involved in and, above all, seeing young lives transformed with varying degrees of success. I loved all of it. Why would I want to do anything else? It wasn't always easy, and often fraught with challenges, but it was also so rewarding. But slowly all that would change.

Perhaps there were early signs in my childhood that pointed to this calling God was laying before me. Most seven- or eight-year-old boys at that time in the 1960s would play cops and robbers or cowboys and Indians, running around chasing one another with makeshift guns or swords or bows and arrows. I did too, lost in imaginary adventures up and down our street, in and out of people's front gardens, and the occasional building site we trespassed on. But I also 'played' at being a priest. We had a large concrete flower trough in the garden that I pretended was an altar, like the one in the Catholic church we attended then as a family. I would borrow by mum's cookbook stand and put our family Bible on it, positioning both on the trough and making out I was leading a church service. There would even be a cup centred precariously on the earth in the bed for 'Communion'. It felt natural and ordinary. Perhaps His whisper was already being formed in my subconscious; those words, yet unspoken, that would ring in my ears in a church service I was invited to many years later that would become my own Damascus Road encounter.

But, returning to my teaching days, such a possibility as becoming a priest was a million miles away from my horizon and not even remotely on my radar. Even when, soon after Sheryl and I were married, someone at church randomly commented, 'Have you ever thought of becoming a vicar?', I hotly dismissed it outright, then and there, without even a second's thought. I was pursuing a teaching career and that was that.

We took a school party to Austria on an educational visit, and I managed to arrange for my family to come too. Our two children, who were still young then, were made such a fuss of by the pupils on this trip, involving them in their games, carrying them on their shoulders, holding their hands as we walked up mountain footpaths. The trip went extremely well; so much so, we arranged for a return visit the following year with the next cohort.

A week before our departure, with everything arranged, the unthinkable happened. I was playing in a charity football match at the school with staff and pupils, and towards the end of the game, I landed awkwardly having jumped up for the ball. I had ruptured a cruciate ligament in my knee and was rolling around on the ground in agony. Everyone there thought I was play-acting to claim a penalty, and one of the pupils even grabbed my injured leg and began tugging at it. It was then, amid my screams, they realised it was serious. The long and the short of it was, that for me, the school trip was over, and I would spend the next six weeks immobilised and on crutches.

It was throughout this period that God clearly spoke to me and began to plant seeds of ministry in my heart; seeds I had not previously considered or entertained as a possibility; but here and now, He had my undivided attention. I argued for a compromise; to do some form of lay ministry but remain in teaching.

This was in a way endorsed when a visiting Christian youth worker at the school later came up to me and told me that he was reading the newspaper and all he could see in front of him were the words, 'Henry – Lay Reader', and asked if that meant anything to me. These words were not physically printed on the sheet, but they would not go from his thoughts until he shared them with me. And so, I was accepted and trained as a Lay Reader in the Church of England. And I thought that was that.

But a good friend of mine, whose spiritual advice I respected, pulled me up soon after and said, 'Don't be surprised if that is not the end of it. There is more to come.'

God had not finished with His intentions for me, but again I found myself not really paying attention. And so, an unexpected occurrence immobilised me in the same way as before, only this time for a longer period. It was just a kickabout in the park with my son. Nothing strenuous, nothing dramatic or taxing. I was simply running for the ball and braked suddenly. Only my knee did not embrace the sudden halt, and this time the cruciate ligament in the same knee as before totally severed.

After reconstructive surgery, I was laid up for months. He had my attention again, and now He was clearly leading me down the path of priesthood; not only in my own thoughts, but through people who would visit me. Repeatedly I heard the same words being echoed: 'I am calling you to priesthood.' The rest is history.

Paul, too, was laid up, immobilised, waiting. He then had a visitor. Ananias was a disciple of Jesus when God spoke to him with a message for Paul. But Ananias was extremely uncomfortable with this instruction and reluctant to comply. He knew of Paul's reputation and no doubt feared for his life. But Ananias, despite his reservations, chose to obey the word and found Paul just as instructed. As he laid hands on him, '*something like scales*' fell from Paul's eyes and his sight was fully restored (Acts 9:18). He rose and was baptised. He was given a new direction and new commission: to bear the name of Jesus before the Gentiles, before kings and before the people of Israel – and, in the process, he would suffer much.

Having recuperated and after spending time in the company of the disciples in Damascus, Paul set out on this mission that would open all kinds of opportunities to plant churches in many areas and regions and to witness before all manner of religious and political audiences.

I was called to ministry after committing my life to Jesus, but not immediately. It came in stages. When I look back, I am not sure I would have launched into any form of ministry straight after committing my life to Him; nor would I have been ready to do so, spiritually or experientially. God had some refining and detoxing to work through in me before I was open to any suggestion of engaging in what would eventually follow.

We are all on journeys through the many corridors of life. We each have our own story to tell. God has a purpose for us even though we may not be conscious of His presence at work in us. We may not be ready to respond to His call. Not until we are able to do so in the manner He chooses. His timing is critical and always perfect. Of that we can be sure.

Thought break

- What does your story look like? Are you someone who likes to branch out into new ventures or stay safe in a familiar and safe routine?

- God can sometimes show up in unexpected ways and present uncomfortable challenges to our way of life. Have there been times in your life's journey where you have experienced something you did not expect that changed your course? How did you react?

- How would you respond to someone who came across very negatively and even aggressively towards your faith in Jesus? What could be your approach in helping them rethink their position of hostility and rejection?

2

By Him, Through Him, with Him

Who do you understand Jesus to be? That may or may not be an obvious question. On one occasion, Jesus asked His disciples who people were saying He was. Several replies came back: 'So they said, "Some *say* John the Baptist, some Elijah, and others Jeremiah or one of the prophets"' (Matthew 16:14). Two things strike me with their reply.

First, they identified Jesus with significant individuals from the past. It is interesting how often people think of Jesus as a historical figure who once was. He was a healer, or a miracle worker, an inspiring teacher, an incredibly wise man, or a prophet. I suspect there are some whose relationship with Jesus is based in the past tense rather than the here and now; where the emphasis is more on what He has done before rather than what He is doing now.

Even in personal testimonies of how God is blessing people's lives and impacting them, there can be a reliance on encounters from way back that perhaps touched them or changed their life in some way through provision, new direction or miraculous healing and the like. Faith can then be shaped and influenced by the past rather than the present.

The second thing that strikes me is that we can base our

understanding of who Jesus is on other people's perceptions and experiential encounters, without really owning it for ourselves. But we do not simply follow a set of doctrinal beliefs, nor are we called to blindly commit our lives to an ideology. We are called to engage with a person, who was and is and always will be – Jesus Christ. He is the eternal Son of God, the One in whom we have our reason for being.

Thomas, for whatever reason, was not present when Jesus appeared to the disciples following His resurrection. So when the others enthusiastically shared their good news with him, you can probably guess the emotions and thoughts going through his mind.

There is nothing more infuriating than missing out on something and having your friends show up with excitement and exuberance, sharing graphically what you let pass you by. 'Hey, man, you should have been there. You really missed out, big time. Where were you, anyway? We've got to tell you, it was awesome...'

You have probably been on the receiving end of such a situation and the last thing you need is to have someone lay it on with spades. All kinds of questions run through your mind, as may have been the case for Thomas. 'Are they exaggerating? Are they fooling with me? After all, that is surely not possible, is it? Maybe they are making it up just to wind me up. Why on earth wasn't I there? Then I would have known for sure.' And the thoughts run on and, as they do, doubt starts to take root, shaping our response.

Thomas' scepticism got the better of him and he could not accept what he was hearing.

> The other disciples therefore said to him, 'We have seen the Lord.'
> So he said to them, 'Unless I see in His hands the print of the nails, and put my finger into the print of the nails, and put my hand into His side, I will not believe.'
> *John 20:25*

Our faith in Jesus cannot be built on the experiences of others, however plausible, convincing or inviting that may sound. We must encounter His presence for ourselves, otherwise the journey of faith becomes a 'blind faith' exercise, where there is no relational anchor to secure it.

It may be fine when everything is going well, and we have a healthy support network around us and there is little demand placed on us. But that can be a dangerous place to be, giving us a false sense of security, because in such an environment we do not grow or mature in our faith, which then remains shallow. When things get rough, there are no deep-set roots in that relationship to hold us fast amid the storms or unexpected changes of circumstances in our lives that can derail us. What happens to our faith then?

Some abandon it, because they lose trust in God, whom they may feel is unable to carry them through the difficulties. Instead, they return to relying on an earthly perspective; to muddle on, with disappointment or disillusionment and perhaps even resentment. Jesus never promised that the walk with Him would be easy or hazard free. He only promised that He would walk with us and lead us through.[19]

Maybe this is where Jesus was leading His disciples in this conversation concerning His identity, because He then turned the question around and directed it at them, asking who they understood Him to be. 'He said to them, "But who do you say that I am?"' (Matthew 16:15). It is a good question to ask yourself, as you pause to consider your own understanding of Jesus.

During an Alpha course[20] we were once running, exploring the Christian faith with a varied group of people, I asked a question along the lines of, 'How would you describe Jesus and what does He mean to you?' The variety of answers and perceptions that came back was staggering and quite revealing.

So, who do you say that He is?

---

[19] John 14:16-18.
[20] Alpha.org.uk (accessed 8th May 2023).

Peter gave Jesus a definitive answer. 'Simon Peter answered and said, "You are the Christ, the Son of the living God"' (Matthew 16:16). And the rest of the disciples probably nodded in agreement with acknowledgements that they were going to say the same or the like. Perhaps that too is your answer to the question I asked. He is the Christ. He is the Son of the living God. Yes, and amen. But what does that mean for us?

More than ever, today, in this uncertain and fragile world we live in, we need to fully understand why Jesus is so significant and important in our lives. We need to be able to convey that certainty to a lost world that I believe is open and searching for a tangible truth that has a strong foundation in a world that is in flux. Following Jesus is a relationship of total commitment. He calls us to follow Him for who He is. He is the eternal Son of God. That is who we are encouraged to follow, not a historical figure who once was and who we remember as someone from the past who demonstrated great things, taught great things and accomplished great things.

If that were the case, then our current relationship with Jesus would be based on upholding the memory of Him as an inspiring role model we look to and try to emulate. But we must not reduce our relationship with Him to such an impersonal and impoverished level. He is alive and reigns here and now. He died, yes, but He also rose from the dead and is now seated on the throne of grace, far above all authority and power that this universe contains; visible and invisible.

Let us stop there for a moment and remind ourselves who it is we are talking about here. For me, the most amazing description of who Jesus is comes in Paul's letter to the Colossians, and that is where we are going now to explore and discover some breath-taking truths about Him. Paul writes:

> He is the image of the invisible God, the firstborn over all creation. For by Him all things were created that are in heaven and that are on earth, visible and invisible, whether thrones or dominions or principalities or powers. All things were created through Him and for

> Him. And He is before all things, and in Him all things
> consist. And He is the head of the body, the church, who
> is the beginning, the firstborn from the dead, that in all
> things He may have the preeminence.
> *Colossians 1:15-18*

Notice it starts by saying 'He is', not 'He was'. We must not look on this with a linear notion of time, or from the perspective of 'that was then, this is now, and one day… who knows'. God is outside time. He created time along with everything else. Time, therefore, is in Him, not He in time. He is the God of the present; of the 'now' not the 'has been'.

John's Gospel highlights this very issue in quite a profound way. It was an occasion when Jesus was confronted by the religious leaders, who were accusing Him of bearing witness to Himself and of being demon possessed. The conversation turned to Abraham and the question of eternal life. His listeners were growing more enraged as the heated discussion went on.

> Then the Jews said to Him, 'Now we know that You
> have a demon! Abraham is dead, and the prophets; and
> You say, "If anyone keeps My word he shall never taste
> death." Are you greater than our father Abraham, who
> is dead? And the prophets are dead. Who do you make
> Yourself out to be?'
> *John 8:52-53*

Jesus then turns the heat up further when things are already at boiling point:

> 'Your father Abraham rejoiced to see My day, and he saw
> *it* and was glad.'
> Then the Jews said to Him, 'You are not yet fifty years
> old, and have You seen Abraham?'
> *John 8:56-57*

And then came the bombshell.

> Jesus said to them, 'Most assuredly, I say to you, before Abraham was, I AM.'
> *John 8:58*

No, it's not a grammatical error or mixing of tenses. Jesus was clearly referring to Himself in terms of God. This is God's name; His identity, as He once explained to Moses, for him to tell the Israelites when they asked who had sent him to them:

> And God said to Moses, 'I AM WHO I AM.' And He said, 'Thus you shall say to the children of Israel, "I AM has sent me to you."'
> *Exodus 3:14*

God's name is His nature. He is 'I AM', not 'I was' or 'I will be'. His presence is everything, because it is in the present that He reveals Himself to us; in the immediacy of now, in our current walk with Him; not in what was or what might be.

Many people look back to the past, with a longing to what was before: 'If only it could be like that now; things were so much better then.' Others set their sights on a future hope, with a wishful conviction that 'one day' everything will be OK, and they just need to somehow get through this bit. By living our lives yearning for the past or longing for the future, we miss the reality of the present and lose sight of His presence with us now.

He is the bookends of time because all time is held in Him; the same before, now and forever.[21] All areas of time are, as it were, rolled into one, in that He is ever present in the now; always was, always will be. The present is the reality He occupies. Eternity does not have a clock. Think about this for a moment. We can only exist in the present. You live now. Yesterday has gone and no longer exists. Tomorrow has not arrived yet. We may have memories of what was and hopes of what is still to come, but it is in the present that we exist.

Our hope in Jesus is in the present because it continues into

---

[21] Revelation 1:8.

a future that is eternal; an eternity that cannot be measured. It is in the 'now' that we are called to discover the God of love who draws near and beckons us to follow Him.

In Him is everything

We are created to be in relationship with God. But it is difficult to relate to someone or identify with them when we can't see them. We cannot really be in relationship with an ideology or a philosophy, but equally we can struggle to have faith in a person who is unseen and seemingly beyond reach. It's perhaps why people find it hard to believe in a God with whom they cannot tangibly connect.

This is one of the reasons why Jesus became a man and entered our world physically. Paul describes Him as the 'image of the invisible God' (Colossians 1:15). Jesus enables us to relate to God through who He is. He is the tangible, expressive face of God with whom we can identify, because He walked among us as a person we could relate to. It is only through Him that we can form a meaningful relationship with God. Everything belongs to Jesus as the only begotten Son of God. Did you know that? Everything. Paul says Jesus is the 'firstborn over all creation' (Colossians 1:15). My understanding is that in Jewish tradition, the firstborn son inherited everything from his father: the whole estate; wealth, livestock, land, servants and workers, as well as his authority.

As firstborn, therefore, Jesus is Lord of all creation. He was not created by God because He is God and as such was there at the start, bringing all things into being. In John's Gospel, we read these words: 'In the beginning was the Word, and the Word was with God, and the Word was God' (John 1:1). Jesus is that Word described here. In Him, through Him, by Him, for Him; the whole of creation exists (Colossians 1:16). 'Then God said, "Let there be…"' (for example, Genesis 1:3,6,14). When He spoke, it materialised; it all came about: the whole universe.

From the smallest speck of dust or atomic particle to the vast expanse of the universe; the whole cosmos. Every solar system, every galaxy, black hole, planet, moon and star. Whatever is out there, He made. Things that are invisible as well as visible, and that includes things we are not even aware are there. The spiritual world as well as the physical one, both equally real and co-existing. Every power, principality and authority, including all the laws of science: physics, chemistry, biology, zoology and every other ology. Mathematics, gravity, time. Wow! Can you get your head around that? It is worth saying again. Everything that exists, He created it all; and you and me, made in His image and likeness, as the pinnacle of His creation.

As if that is not enough to blow our minds, not only did He make it all and set its foundations in place with clearly defined structures and parameters, but He is not restricted by any of it. He created gravity but walks on water. He created the weather but tells the storms to back off. He created mathematics but multiplies food to feed thousands from five loaves and two fish. He created our frail and fragile bodies with all our complexities and peculiarities, prone to sickness, disease and deterioration, but can restore and replace body parts, heal every ailment or disease, and even bring back to life what has died. Jesus is not bound by His creation nor confined by it.

That is why 'He is before all things, and in Him all things consist' (Colossians 1:17). Everything that exists, exists in Him. Nothing can exist outside Him. He holds all things in His hand… everything. He unites everything that there is and gives it its functionality and purpose in the universe. Nothing is random or by chance because everything has a proper place in His design. Without Him there is nothing. He sustains all life and brings it all together. Whatever He lets go of ceases to be.

This is the Jesus we are describing who called disciples to follow Him and calls you and me to do likewise. That brings us to the next point Paul draws out in this passage, one that embraces each one of us as the centre of His focus and attention.

Paul describes Jesus as 'the head of the body, the church'

(Colossians 1:18). Jesus is not separate from, but one with us when He calls us to follow Him. Because of who He is, as we have just described above, He wants us to 'be filled with all the fullness of God' living in us (Ephesians 3:19). Everything that is of God, He pours into you and me. As physically the head and the body are inseparably one, so too is what is envisaged here. His life-giving presence flows within us. His power and authority rest upon us and His love is released through us.

When we surrender our lives to Jesus, we become part of His body, the Church. It is an organism, not an organisation. He comes to dwell in us when we invite Him into our lives. 'Jesus answered and said to him, "If anyone loves Me, he will keep My word; and My Father will love Him, and We will come to him and make Our home with him"' (John 14:23).

Only a God of love has the desire to come Himself in intimacy to be with us and reside in us, with all His power and might and majesty and mind-blowing glory. The God who is beyond comprehension makes Himself real and accessible to you and me. Could there be more? Yes, there is more!

Becoming part of His body is not some kind of external event, like joining a club or society. There is something even greater that takes place. 'The Spirit Himself bears witness with our spirit that we are children of God' (Romans 8:16). You and I, as the body of Christ, also become children of God. Why is that so significant? Because if we are God's children then by default, we also become 'heirs ... and joint heirs' with Jesus (Romans 8:17). Everything that belongs to Him is ours too, isn't it? That is surely what being a joint heir implies, because the body does not inherit anything that does not also belong to the head, does it?

He sealed that on the cross when He took back all the legitimate and legal claims from the enemy and reconciled us to Himself. So the deal from His perspective is, I envisage, something like this: 'When you give Me everything you have, I will give you everything I have.'

Now, what could we possibly give God that He does not

already own? He even owns our sin. Did you know that? Jesus took our sin upon Himself as if it were His sin and nailed it to the cross on which He died. It was buried with Him in the grave. Set free from that sin and reconciled with God, we now share in His inheritance. That is the nature of being one with Him as His body. Everything He has, He releases to us.

Let me return to the notion of time which I mentioned earlier. Paul moves on in this passage to describe Jesus as 'the beginning, the firstborn from the dead' (Colossians 1:18). He died and was buried, yes. But three days later He was raised from the dead. He rose and vanquished death. That means death now belongs to Him and He can do with it what He likes. He has turned death from an end-of-the-line terminus to a gateway into eternal life.

Eternity is His domain. He walks in its corridors. Not only does He own creation, but everything beyond it too. We do not know what eternity looks like. It inhabits no concept of time we can comprehend. Scientists might give it a theoretical explanation, but no one this side of the grave has experienced its reality. It is through Jesus, as the beginning and the firstborn, who opened eternal life to us, that we can enter the reality of what it means to enjoy and be enveloped in God's love forever.

The final thing Paul describes here is 'that in all things He may have the preeminence' (Colossians 1:18). In other words, Jesus has no equal; He is first in all things. He has the supremacy, the sovereignty, and reigns over all things and all circumstances. His name is higher than any other name.[22] Whatever name is given to everything that exists, the name of Jesus is higher, is sovereign over and is greater than. It means His name is higher than the name of every pandemic; every sickness and disease that is medically named and identified; every form of cancer, of heart disease, of dementia, of epilepsy, of MS and ME; add your own medical condition. His name is greater than every mental health issue and disorder. It is above

---

[22] Philippians 2:9-11.

the names of depression, anxiety, fear, poverty, redundancy, unemployment, economic recession. It is more powerful than every chain of addiction that binds and enslaves the human spirit, be it drug abuse, alcoholism, pornography, gambling, gluttony, greed, and the like. His name breaks the chain of every other name that binds or restricts our lives.

When we discover who Jesus really is, we can no longer treat Him with indifference, complacency, as a feel-good add-on, as an appendage to our busy lives with a once-a-week get-together, or as customer services when things go wrong. We need to rediscover that sense of awe and wonder and to come before Him in reverence and fear. He deserves and demands nothing less.

No wonder His disciples were so often awestruck and dumbfounded at the display of His authority and influence over everything. I wonder if in our modern society we have lost the sense of reverence for who God is because our world has squeezed Him out and continues to do so. Perhaps at times our outward religious endeavours have lost sight of the greatness of God and His significance in our lives.

When we know who He is, it enlarges who we become. But we need to be clear where such revelation comes from. We cannot create God in our image but must embrace our relationship with Him on His terms and by His provenance. As Jesus pointed out to Peter in Matthew 16:17, it was divine revelation rather than human understanding that led this disciple to acknowledge who Jesus was in this way. What followed was a profound declaration of what such faith releases.

> And I also say to you that you are Peter, and on this rock I will build My church, and the gates of Hades shall not prevail against it. And I will give you the keys of the kingdom of heaven, and whatever you bind on earth will be bound in heaven, and whatever you loose on earth will be loosed in heaven.
> *Matthew 16:18-19*

The Church Jesus is building is established on the knowledge and confession of who He is, and this is the rock on which our faith is firmly grounded. It is this conviction, revealed to us by the Father through the Holy Spirit, that becomes our firm foundation and deep-rootedness.

This is the Church that can carry the weight of His presence, authority and power into our communities. This is the Church that becomes unstoppable, whereby nothing can stand in her way, and nothing can remain shut before the advancement of His kingdom. This is the Church that is given access to the resources of heaven and released through Him.

It begins with bowing before Him and truly recognising who He is and then recognising who He has called us to become. We are not called to sit on a fence of uncertainty. We must step onto the path of His promise, in trust and surrender, wherever it leads us, wherever He takes us.

Road of encounter

Understanding this truth is not an academic exercise but a road of discovery He takes us on. It is in the time we spend with Him that such revelation is increasingly experienced by us who follow Him. There may be times when we are not even aware of His presence, but He is there constantly.

After Jesus' death and burial, the word had spread that He was alive, that He had risen from the dead. Some women encountered Him in the garden where His tomb lay empty, the stone rolled away and the Roman soldiers placed to guard it slumped on the ground, paralysed with fear. Some of His disciples were sceptical about the news and had to go and see for themselves. It was just as the women had described. He was not there. He was alive![23]

At around that time, two of Jesus' disciples were travelling to Emmaus, a small village some seven miles outside Jerusalem.

---

[23] Matthew 28:1-8; John 20:1-9.

They had heard the rumours and, not having witnessed it themselves, were full of questions. News like that travels and as it does, versions can get distorted. Who said what to whom? Who saw for themselves? Who told you and how do they know for sure? As the two of them walked along the road, they would have been talking through what they had heard and the possible implications that would ensue from this revelation. They must have been so engrossed in their conversation, perhaps gesticulating with arms waving, uncertainty generating from the possibilities such news might imply, that they failed to notice someone else appear and walk alongside them, subtly drawing closer and listening in.

Have you been to one of those parties where you're deep in conversation with one or two others over some controversial issue in the news, where everyone has their own opinion and solution, and then someone else joins in, seemingly unnoticed at first, just listening? They are at first ignored as the conversation continues, and then eventually this stranger asks you all what you are talking about and drops in a contribution to the debate that stuns and silences everyone.

I suggest something like this happened on this road, and the stranger, unbeknown to them, was Jesus Himself. He entered the conversation, in an inquisitive manner, seeming to know nothing about the news they were discussing. 'What kind of conversation *is* this that you have with one another as you walk and are sad?' (Luke 24:17).

Isn't it annoying when news you are sharing, and expecting others to know about and empathise with, doesn't get the reaction you expect? It's as if the 'outsider' is blasé about what you embrace so passionately. 'What do you mean you don't know?' So you go through the whole process of explaining, perhaps with a tone of derision, the things that to you are so obvious. Then, like the stranger at the party bringing their own contribution to the debate, Jesus threw in the profound reality of not only acknowledging that He was aware of the circumstances, but also going deeper with them through

Scripture, expanding on the reasons for and necessity of all that had taken place.

They still didn't know His identity when they reached their destination at the end of the day, but they were impressed enough to invite Him to stay with them, so engrossed were they with His profound explanations. Something new was stirring in them, but the penny did not drop until He broke bread with them, and before they could react, 'He vanished from their sight' (Luke 24:29-31).

Hindsight is always a marvellous thing. We are all full of wisdom and understanding then, when all is revealed, wondering why it did not 'click' beforehand. Sometimes unexpected things trigger the reality in us, and the 'light bulb' comes on.

It was then, in the breaking of the bread, that these two disciples comprehended the fire that had burned in them as Jesus unpacked so much and revealed such profound things to them along the road. It was then that the reality of His presence dawned on them, whereby they dropped everything and raced back to confirm to the other disciples all they had experienced.

There are many roads we travel on in our lives, and many opportunities for Him to draw alongside us so we may encounter His presence. We do not always recognise it until some profound revelation awakens us to the truth that He continually walks with us and engages with us. Perhaps, when we experience that encounter, like those two on the road, we want to hurriedly share that with others, confirming His living reality among us here and now.

Thought break

- How big is 'your' God and how do you identify with Him?

- Look again at Paul's description of Jesus in Colossians 1:15-18. Is this the Jesus you recognise from your own experience, or are there surprises you were maybe not fully aware of or conscious of? If so, what are they and how do they enrich your understanding of who He is?

- How close do you feel Jesus is in the ordinary and everyday experiences of your life? What about when things appear tough or pressurised? Where or when have you experienced His presence most or least? Why might that be so?

3

Following with Intent

When I retired from ministry as a parish priest in 2019, the perception Sheryl and I had had of what stepping down would entail and what it might look like quickly evaporated through the circumstances that were to follow; circumstances which God had His hand on and directed throughout.

After a period of settling, nesting and resting in our new home and the community where we were led to in Braintree, a town not far from Chelmsford in mid-Essex, we began to sense a stirring that echoed back to something God had said to us in the process of discerning the post-retirement agenda. It was in the words, 'I need you in Braintree,' which we felt God had spoken to us. That may sound quite arrogant, but our relationship with Jesus has matured enough to recognise the sense of when God is speaking to us and when He is not. We have learned from experience to take Him at His word fully, even if at times it sounds strange, outrageous or incomprehensible. What He says, He always follows up, with confirmation and fulfilment that acknowledges the validity of His word. We have learned to follow what He says until He says otherwise, even if we are not always sure where it's leading us. It often does not take us long to discover His purpose in it.

Not only is God's word true and valid, but it is also timely. After our move, and having already been diagnosed with cancer, I was still under the healthcare of my previous hospital, now two to three hours' drive away. It was not straightforward to continue with that arrangement, especially as the consultant was urging me to have what he deemed as necessary surgery, and was persistent in his reminders for me to decide and proceed swiftly. It would have meant months of difficult journeys, to-ing and fro-ing in the process. We did not jump in. We were at peace with the situation and not daunted or fearful of the outcome. The fact that God had clearly stated He had a purpose for us both in Braintree underpinned what we decided to do next.

It was the opposite of what my team of doctors were recommending. Please do not misunderstand: I am not advocating ignoring sound medical advice and under normal circumstances we would have followed their counsel. But, on this occasion, conviction that God had a different path led us to trust in His prompting. It was a decision that was to prove right.

Having registered with the local health centre, as you do, I requested that my case be transferred to the hospital near where we now lived. There I could pursue the same course of treatment more locally and be in a better position for postoperative recovery, which in my circumstance would have been lengthy.

Notice I said *would have*. The process of referral was so swift, I was seeing a new consultant in a short space of time. I wasn't expecting this but welcomed it. The hospital had acquired all my previous notes and test results and were also conducting some of their own tests.

Sitting in front of the consultant, Sheryl and I felt confident and peaceful, even as he mulled through all the paperwork and charts in front of him. He turned backwards and forwards through them and then to his computer screen and the MRI scans that appeared, with puzzling expressions appearing on his face at every glance, as he conversed with his team sitting with him in a language only the medically trained can understand.

He then looked at us and informed us that, in his opinion,

surgery would be like smashing a nut with a sledgehammer and unnecessary, because the cancer was small and slow-growing. He would put me on active surveillance and monitor the situation regularly.

Sheryl and I looked at each other and smiled, and when we left the meeting, we hugged one another and punched the air. How gracious our God is, to not put me through unnecessary procedures with all the ensuing complications that would result. Further scans and tests that have since followed confirmed the consultant's decision to be right.

Was the first hospital's diagnosis wrong, or did God simply intervene in the severity of my condition? We will never know. We do not need to. All we need to know is that God had other plans, and this was not going to misdirect His purpose for us.

In the first few months of living in Braintree, we visited as many local churches as we could find, to get the feel of each one and discern where God wanted us to settle and call our spiritual home. It was His idea and directive, not ours, and we were not to stop visiting until He specifically told us to. Some places were clearly not for us; others we returned to a few times, not quite sure how we might 'fit in', knowing God had plans to use us.

In that time, we kept passing a church in our street, two minutes' walk from our house. From the outside it did not look like anything was going on there. Eventually we stepped in, and what we experienced blew us away. The worship taking place was inspirational. The atmosphere was one of encounter on a deep and profound level. We were welcomed with such warmth, you would have thought we were part of that fellowship already. We made sure we maintained our anonymity as church leaders, as we had in all the churches we visited. We walked out at the end of the service, full of excitement and anticipation, thinking surely this was where God intended us to settle; it had our DNA written all over it and we would feel very happy there.

We thought that was it, when God pulled us up short, with a clear, 'Did I tell you to stop? You carry on until I tell you otherwise.' We were to continue our 'churches tour' for a further few months, until finally He brought us back to this church we had fallen in love with – Elim Braintree (ECB) – and the words of confirmation we so wanted to hear: 'This is now to be your spiritual home.' It was significant that we were obedient to His voice and instruction because we are called to follow Him, not He us.

We had visited all the local churches, and in doing so got a feel of the area and the spiritual temperature of the community, discovering its strengths and weaknesses in the process. It might help you to know at this point that our spiritual DNA and mindset is not denominationally restricted, and we have a heart for ecumenical unity in the gospel and seeing the kingdom of God influence and transform our communities at a local level. In our time leading the church at Rainham, where we ministered before retiring to Braintree, we engaged with many of the various denominations there, and were involved in a lot of ministering together as an ecumenical movement we called 'One Church'. We saw many blessings spring from that unity and many strong relationships built across the churches. We were familiar and comfortable with the different styles of worship we were invited to participate in, and the same was true in our reciprocation as hosts. There was a strong bond between all the church leaders, and to this day we remain in touch with some of them. This remains part of our heart, even in our current setting.

Fruitful gateways

By its very nature, following involves movement. You cannot follow and remain where you are. You must venture out and take a course into uncharted territory; into a future that is held by Jesus, even if it is, at the outset, unknown to you. Change therefore is inevitable and necessary.

It is a change not only in direction but in identity as well. I can no longer remain where I am, nor can I remain who I am. Everything alters. My perspective, my perception, my priorities and my vision. What I start out in shifts as the journey progresses, and my understanding of who I am and who He is enlarges and comes more into focus. Transformation is the desire of God's heart for each one of us.

As the time was drawing closer and His final hours were looming large before Him, Jesus spent crucial time with His disciples, teaching and discoursing with them in order to prepare them for what was to come. These bite-size nuggets would enable His disciples not only to comprehend but also to be equipped for all that lay ahead for them after He had gone through the agonies that awaited Him, and returned to His heavenly Father in His full glory.

So much packed into so short a space of time. We read this in John 13 to 16; the reinforced commandment to love one another, the promise of another helper, the indwelling relationship of Father and Son and the gift of His peace, the intimacy and inseparable nature of their relationship with Him, the work of His Holy Spirit that would follow and so much more.

Jesus told the disciples that He was going on ahead to make things ready so He could come back and take them to be where He would be. He began by encouraging them not to be anxious or troubled but to trust Him.[24] Is it just me, or do you also find your heart skips a beat whenever someone starts off by saying to you, 'Now I don't want you to be worried or upset, but…' We often think bad news is coming. At least, I do.

It appears the inference that Jesus would soon be leaving them was unsettling those gathered, as Thomas, somewhat confused, asked Jesus to explain because he did not know where Jesus was going and needed to know the way. Perhaps they all needed the security of knowing what was ahead and how to continue the pathway they were on, in need of some kind of 'compass' to do so. Jesus then gave them a clear 'road map' that was profound and clear cut: 'Jesus said to him, "I am the way,

---

[24] John 14:1-4.

the truth, and the life. No one comes to the Father except through Me'" (John 14:6).

There are two things in this statement that have strong implications for all of us who are called to follow. Both speak in terms of relationship and identity. They define the nature of the pathway we are to undertake and the destination we are heading towards. In both cases they are revelations that single out unmistakably the nature of God and the unique way He can be discovered and followed.

First, Jesus calls *Himself* 'the way, the truth, and the life'. To a world that is sceptical of any singular notion of absolute meaning, direction or identity, this may sound absurd and even inflammatory, because the world can only relate to multiple truths and varied ways to find fulfilment and enlightenment; each as valid as the next. Each has a voice, and each is trying to shout louder than the other voices.

So what was so profound and singular about Jesus' words? Jesus did not say, 'Hey, guys, I know the way we should go,' or, 'I can give you a map and a set of instructions of how to get you there.' He did not say, 'I know about truth,' or, 'I can teach you the truth.' He did not say, 'I know all about life,' or, 'I can show you how to best go about your lives.' He was precise in His wording. He *is* the way. He *is* the truth. He *is* the life. He does not reveal those things. He *is* those things.

The pathway we are placed on lies *in Him*, not in an external religious route that points to Him. He is not a satnav to a destination. He is the destination and takes us to complete that destined route, all the way to the very heart of God, our heavenly Father.

It is in Him, it is through Him, it is with Him that we are called to follow. Unless we are in that kind of relationship with Him in every sense of the intimacy it invokes, we will miss the whole point of discipleship in Him, and never fulfil that which He wants us to grow in.

The second thing Jesus said in that statement relates to His uniqueness in being the only means by which we can be saved from the corrosive and destructive nature of sin. He is the only way we can discover and enter a right relationship with God. In essence, no one can find their way to the Father unless they go through Him.

That blows smoke in the eyes of every other pathway by which people seek to find fulfilment, and more importantly justification with, a creator God who made us in His image and likeness and from whom humanity rebelled and went their own way, steeped in the sin that disempowered us from knowing the fullness of life.

Here is the misunderstanding we can often live under. It does not matter how or who we, in our imaginations, perceive God to be. It is irrelevant how we, through our contemplations, doctrines, theological insights or philosophies construct an image of who we interpret God to be, and then proceed to build our religious frameworks around that.

What matters, and what Jesus clearly spells out to us here, is what God says. If I tell you where I live and how to get to my house and you choose to ignore what I say and decide I live in a different place and then unsuccessfully attempt to find me living there, how foolish is that?

If God says, 'This is who I am and this is how to find me; in fact, this is the only possible way you can find me,' why would we choose to ignore what He says and opt for something else that will never in a million years get us to the destination He can lead us to? It makes no sense. It is disastrous to even begin down such a route, knowing there is a clear and visible direction found only in Jesus.

> Enter by the narrow gate; for wide *is* the gate and broad *is* the way that leads to destruction, and there are many who go in by it. Because narrow *is* the gate and difficult *is* the way which leads to life, and there are few who find it.
> *Matthew 7:13-14*

Why is finding His narrow path so difficult to do, whereas the wider universal road is so well trodden? I believe for the very reasons expressed above. We find it easier to make God in our own image and to follow the illusion we construct, which places little or no demand upon us, in blissful unawareness of the destructive route it is taking, rather than surrendering to the voice that calls us in love to follow Him.[25]

We cannot live under the deception that somehow all roads and pathways, however crooked and unstable, however dodgy and misguided, somehow lead us to God and in the end the slate is wiped clean regardless. That makes a mockery of His sacrifice on the cross; the payment once offered for all, for our redemption.

It is perhaps why Jesus said to His disciples that to follow Him is sacrificial and costly. It takes self out of the equation and puts Him at the centre of our lives. We die to self so that He might live in us. You can gain the whole world and all the riches it possesses and still be lost in eternity, as is made clear in Matthew 16:24-26. It is the difficult choice to make, but the right choice.

That is easier said than done, because we have so many trappings, so many distractions and seductive pulls in our lives and we so easily succumb to the myriad of temptations we face every day for a more comfortable, self-centred lifestyle. If we are honest, we still want to be in control, to be our own lord, and for God to be an accessory at the beckon of convenience should we choose to call upon Him, but who has no direct effect or influence upon our lives.

That proves to be a lie and an illusion because we very quickly discover there is no peace or contentment in such a pursuit; only anxiety, pressure, demands and oppressive outcomes that make our lives more complicated, not less. While the world offers us image, only the kingdom of God found in Jesus offers us substance. Contentment, peace and joy can only be found in the source of these experiences – Jesus Himself,

---

[25] John 10:3-5,10.

who brings us these things in exchange for all the negative things we choose to leave with Him when we take up the invitation to follow.[26] We must choose, because there is no provision for compromise here. We choose the 'narrow gate ... which leads to life' or the wide gate which 'leads to destruction'. We do not need to look far to see how the world is destroying itself; society is fragmented and insecure, relationships are brittle and crumbling. We do not need to look far to see that religion devoid of relationship is either losing its grip on humankind (if it ever had one), or is becoming fundamentalist at one extreme or complacent and indifferent at the other. That may sound like an oversimplification, inasmuch as many are satisfied with a worldly or religious lifestyle and as such feel 'fulfilled'.

But in terms of eternity and 'salvation', such a world view is short lived and futile and, as such, is heading for disaster; it will not last. Only the kingdom of God has eternal significance and worth. Our materialistic wealth and worldly well-being cannot save us; nor can the faith of others, whether our family, church or believing friends; nor can our external religious observance.

It is like trying to take a whole lot of baggage through a narrow turnstile or attempting to get through with others at the same time. It does not work. It is only our personal response to Jesus' offer of life through His shed blood that enables us entry; without the baggage, which is ditched at the foot of the cross. This is the criterion of following that Jesus alludes to here. This is the challenge He presents us with. 'This is the deal if you want to be where I am.'

Following costs

There will always be those who want both lifestyles: to maintain their own independence from God while at the same time looking to Him for favour and justification, as if in some way it

---

[26] Matthew 11:28-30.

is their right or something God owes them. He owes us nothing. He is the author and creator of life. There is no life apart from Him, and yet we can often belittle the gift of life He gives us, as if it were our entitlement.

Should we presume that life in this universe revolves around us? And yet, at times I suspect we do. We either take our lives for granted in the comfort zones we occupy and presume we have earned our right to be contented with our lot, even if we inevitably strive for more in a self-conscious search for improvement, or we struggle with a life that is far from comfortable and secure, where each day presents its own challenges of survival and where resentment and scepticism fuel our emotional disposition, sometimes generating a spillover of anger or outrage, because we feel our rights in life are ignored or overlooked.

The life Jesus calls us to removes these trappings and puts us in a greater place of security, value and worth; greater than anything the world can offer. But it requires a choice we must make at the outset. We cannot have both. We must decide, because one or the other lifestyle must die.

A rich young ruler once walked up to Jesus, wanting to justify himself before Him. I wonder if it is a human trait in all of us. The desire for approval, recognition or accolade and the need for justification of our lifestyle and actions. It may have been what this stranger was seeking, who knows? After all, he was young and he had wealth; no doubt, a comfortable lifestyle that would have been the envy of many. But perhaps he somehow needed to be commended by Jesus, and so trying to butter Him up with compliments of 'Good Teacher' (Matthew 19:16), he asked a question I suggest he, as a Jew, already knew the answer to, regarding obtaining eternal life and keeping the commandments. Because when Jesus pointed out which ones to keep, this young ruler claimed to already be ticking all the boxes. As was so often the case when these kinds of questions were presented to Jesus, the expected answers didn't come the way the enquirer anticipated. What was he expecting? A pat on the back with perhaps Jesus drawing the crowd's attention to him in approval?

No, he got what he did not expect: 'Jesus said to him, "If you want to be perfect, go, sell what you have and give to the poor, and you will have treasure in heaven; and come, follow Me"' (Matthew 19:21). But he could not. He was trapped in the possessions that possessed him. He not only didn't get what he was hoping for, but, worse still perhaps, went away in disappointment and humiliation before his onlookers, because he couldn't or wouldn't meet the requirements Jesus challenged him with.

This is not so much a matter of material possessions as of attitude of heart. It can be any number of things that possess us or oppress us in our lives, preventing us from moving into the things God wants us to take hold of.

It therefore raises questions about what we hold on to as our means of security and identity, and what we are prepared to let go of or, more significantly, step into. This has significance in our discipleship because it can rule or dominate our focus and attitude in life and become a barrier to the place of intimacy that He has called us to or wants to release in us.

The sad and unfortunate thing is that there are always going to be those who, with every good intention and sincerity, will be full of enthusiasm at voicing their willingness to follow – until they read the small print and then quickly withdraw their commitment, because for them, the cost is too high.

The scribe, for example, who openly declared his allegiance to follow come what may, until Jesus spelt out what that involved. Or the disciple who would follow Him, but not until he was free from other obligations or commitments, until Jesus pressed in with the order of priorities that he must decide on.[27]

The essence of our faith and conditions for following Jesus as His disciples require us to believe in Him to the extent of total trust and surrender to His will. To put it in human

---

[27] Matthew 8:19-22.

relationship terms, think of a couple whose marriage is strong and secure. Their commitment to one another, in this covenant of belonging to each other and being one, is single-minded. They share their lives 24/7. It is built on companionship, trust, reliance on and support for each other.

What would that relationship look like if it were much looser, indifferent and inconsistent, where each went their separate ways with the occasional get-together? On what kind of foundation could such a marital arrangement exist? It is not something a close couple who love each other and are devoted to one another other, excluding all else, would ever consider. That is what Jesus calls us to. That is what we are committed to. It is here that the intimacy of fellowship with Him exists.

Thought break

- What do you feel about change? Do you think God has a purpose for your life, and do you recognise it? How comfortable are you with any movement God may call you to make in the plans He has for you?

- How do you respond to people who say there are many ways to find God and all religions are equal? How far do you agree with Jesus when He says that He is the only way to the Father? What questions does that raise for you?

- Reflect on the encounter the rich young man had with Jesus. What would be your reaction if you were in his place? Are there things or issues that hold you back from the commitment Jesus is asking of you?

4

Essential Grace

When I first committed my life to Jesus, I went through what can only be describe as a honeymoon period. I was full of excitement, even awestruck at the exuberant joy of His outpoured love upon my life. Like a lovesick teenager experiencing first love, everything was fresh and new and yet familiar too.

My parents' faith, which had underpinned my foundational development in those early years of my growing up, took on a whole new identity with an underlying perspective that made more sense than it ever had and, perhaps for the first time, encompassed a reality I had not truly appreciated before.

I joined a local church near where I lived, by invitation of a dear friend and his wife, who were so instrumental in making my encounter with Jesus possible. Everything seemed or felt new. A pioneering spirit grew in me, like that of an early explorer locating an undiscovered land or a scientist finding a hitherto unknown phenomenon, punching the air with shouts of 'Eureka!' I wanted to press into and unearth everything my heartstrings were tugging at concerning this amazing God who showed up with such a life-changing impact. It was unexpected and profound. I was now hungrier than ever to discover more about Him.

I immersed myself in the Bible like someone who had just received the most amazing gift ever and was reading the instructions on how to assemble and use what he had just pulled out of the box; eager and impatient to see it fully functioning. But these words I was reading concerning God and His relationship with us were not so much from a divinely constructed instruction manual. No, this was more like a love letter that thrilled and excited, encouraged and affirmed... and challenged... and questioned my lifestyle. Some of it was going over my head. Other parts leapt out and inspired with 'light bulb' moments of revealed truth.

I was also forming new friendships within the church fellowship I became part of, and was keen to immerse myself more fully in the church's life and witness. It felt like a whole different world I had entered, yet at the same time I was living in the reality of what was still the normal everyday circumstances that were there before. New and old. Unfamiliar and familiar. Daunting yet comfortable. Sacred and secular.

All seemed to merge in an almost seamless thread of experiences that appeared to be shaping a new norm I was at ease with. I was still coming to terms with the feelings and emotions and excitement, while trying to rationalise this journey I was undertaking. It felt surreal and yet not. Perhaps this is what those early disciples felt and experienced who, directly or through others, were drawn into this new journey of discovery.[28] 'Could this be...?' (John 4:29).

It is interesting, isn't it, that whenever we have good news to share which we are ecstatic about and leaping for joy over, we want the world to know. We get the new job we have always wanted; we get engaged to the most loving person ever; we set a date for a wedding; we find out we are about to become a parent; we feel the Lord calling us to ministry, and doors fly open; we have just been given the all-clear over a health scare; we have some really exciting news concerning a significant breakthrough in a family issue; we see an old friend after many years apart; we go on a great holiday. Whatever the reason, good

---

[28] Mark 1:18-20; 2:13-14; John 1:40-42, 45-49.

news cannot be kept to ourselves. We want others to share in what we are experiencing.

Isn't this how we should feel when we discover the intimacy of a loving God who is so crazy about us and wants us to encounter the depth of love that He has for us? We not only want to drop everything and follow Him, but we also want the world to know. We want everyone to discover for themselves what we have just discovered. Isn't that the most natural thing in the world to want to express? So why don't we? What is holding us back? Why isn't the Church shouting this message from the rooftops?

After all, when those first disciples engaged with the multitudes in Jerusalem following their encounter with the Holy Spirit, people were amazed and some at first thought they were drunk. They were uninhibited in the message they proclaimed. They didn't care who heard, officials or not. In fact, they wanted everyone to hear and, amazingly, when they spoke to the crowds, all those gathered miraculously heard them speaking in their own native tongue.[29]

Imagine it. One moment they were ordinary people gathered in an upper room, waiting for the promise Jesus had given them. The next moment, as if from nowhere, they were drenched in His presence. Anticipation grew as the Holy Spirit blew over them like a wind and fanned the embers of their expectation, whereby they ignited, and fire came and impassioned them with boldness. They then went out fearless and couldn't keep quiet, speaking a language all those on the outside understood. How out of the ordinary is that? Yet how real when God shows up.

I wonder sometimes if we were to engage with our community in a manner that was less 'churchy' in its vocabulary with the assumption that people understood, and more in the relational language of love that is kingdom-centred, whether more people would identify with it and respond? We are, after all, called to gather people of all walks of life, nationalities and

---

[29] Acts 2:4-13.

backgrounds to a person, not to an institution.

People were so impressed and so convinced by their passionately delivered message that they 'wanted in' as well. In fact, that day, after hearing Peter's message, thousands of people discovered the love of Jesus for themselves. Passion carries conviction that is infectious. 'Then those who gladly received his word were baptized; and that day about three thousand souls were added *to them*' (Acts 2:41). From then on more and more were added to their number... and the good news continued to spread.

In Acts 5 we read that people were coming to faith, lives were being changed for the better, people were being healed from all kinds of sicknesses and diseases, and others were being set free from all kinds of demonic oppression. And the news of it all was spreading and its impact increasing.

Wow! You cannot keep news like that quiet. You cannot keep that to yourself, whether you've been directly affected or just witnessed it happening. You will want to tell others what you've just seen or experienced. Good news like that travels fast.

Now, I know that how we convey our excitement or enthusiasm over something important to us makes a difference to how others receive it. Have you ever tried to share with your friends, family or work colleagues the excitement of an astonishing and memorable holiday you have just come back from? You want to show them all the hundreds of photos and videos you took and talk them through every moment you experienced and adventure you enjoyed. Within thirty seconds you realise they have switched off and their eyes are gazing elsewhere. Why? Because your experience is not their experience, so you cannot convey in any meaningful way the joy that is inside you, try as you may.

Attempting to share personal memorabilia with disinterested parties is one thing. But what about when it comes to sharing personal encounters with God? That can be a lot more sensitive and precarious, especially when we do not want those on the receiving end to be negatively affected by it.

It was early on in my new-found faith and enthusiasm for Jesus that I first took Sheryl to a gathering at a Christian friend's house, on his invitation. We had not been going out long and everything in our relationship was still fresh and new, as we learned and discovered unfamiliar things about each other. Sheryl at that stage would not have described herself as a Christian (though she was by the time we married). I was careful not to bombard her with my own newly found exuberance, even though I longed to share that joy with her. Our host, on the other hand, was not so restrained.

It was quite a crowded gathering, and Sheryl was only acquainted with a couple of people there. Not long into the evening, our host started to get what I can only describe as 'heavy'. It felt as if Sheryl became the sole target of his overenthusiastic 'Bible bashing' interrogation. I kept trying to divert the subject, but he kept coming back. I was desperate for her not to be put off and run a mile. Perhaps there was an element of divine shielding from any damage that might have derailed God's plans for her life and His purpose for us both. It was, I am pleased to say, an isolated incident.

By taking initiatives ourselves, based on our own zeal and passion rather than being prompted or directed by the Holy Spirit in line with His purposes, not our own, we can sometimes get in the way of what God wants to do Himself.

Phased encounters

It was not long after returning to the busyness of parish life in Rainham, following a sabbatical break that, in 2013, we heard of an outpouring of the Holy Spirit taking place in a church in Cwmbran, South Wales. The leaders there stopped short of calling it a revival, but clearly something profound was going on.

They discerned that it was right to hold meetings in the church every night, and very quickly these were packed continuously as word began to spread and people were coming from all over the world to witness what was happening. Lives were being touched, people were being healed in varying and unbelievable ways, and many were coming to faith in Jesus as a result.

Sheryl and I were both convicted to go and experience this outpouring for ourselves. We booked some time off and spent a few days there. I would not say that outwardly there was anything visibly spectacular as we entered the building. The worship and the preaching were good, but nothing out of the ordinary; nothing we had not heard or experienced before. If anything, the tone was modest and not hyped up. But the spiritual atmosphere in that place when we walked in was like nothing we had encountered anywhere else up until that point. The weight of God's presence was overwhelming, as night after night we were drenched in this heavenly soaking of His love.

Sheryl, who had suffered with chronic arthritis in her hands, was healed, and full movement in the use of her previously restricted fingers was restored. I too was affected in a profound way in my spirit, tangibly manifesting itself in uncontrollable shaking and bobbing up and down; even when I got back to our hotel bed that night, I could not stop. Nor did I want to. I just wanted to absorb the experience.

The trip left a lasting mark on us, but we had a dilemma as we returned to Rainham on such a high. How would we convey what had just happened to a congregation who would not imagine, let alone understand, the profound impact with which God had touched us? This was way beyond sharing holiday snaps with uninterested parties. We decided not to; or rather felt God prompt us not to, but instead to allow Him to do the sharing.

What we had not at that point appreciated was that we had brought back with us an impartation of His presence. When you come close to God in such a way, inevitably it rubs off on you and you carry it, consciously or not. The following Sunday at the morning service, we shared that we had been blessed while in Wales and avoided the need to expand. Instead, we invited people to come forward just for a blessing and anointing with oil if they wanted to. They did, nearly the whole church, and as they came forward, God took over.

There was a visible impact each person was experiencing as they drew close to the front where Sheryl and I were standing to receive them; some in tears, others falling over in the Spirit, overcome with emotion, and clearly touched by God's loving presence. We decided to repeat the invitation to the more 'traditional' evening congregation, not wanting them to miss out. In all honesty, we did not expect them to be touched in the same way; I don't know why. Perhaps it reveals our own limited preconceptions. But God affected them in the same way as in the morning.

In fact, this went on for several weeks. Not just in our services, where we were also beginning to see an increase in healings taking place and a manifestation in the use of spiritual gifts, but in our ecumenical gatherings. Church leaders we were meeting with and praying with were also being anointed. At one such gathering in our church, the chancel area became littered with leaders who were overcome with the Holy Spirit and lay prostrate on the floor, soaking in His presence. They then experienced blessings in their own churches and ministries.

If Jesus is the truth that sets us free, and He is, and in Him we are set free,[30] then what we read about happening on that first Pentecost in Jerusalem should still be happening here and now. I am not suggesting we are not seeing evidence of this today, in many churches and in many places in the world. I would go further and suggest that globally, the Church is growing faster than it ever has. But equally, there are places and, sadly, churches where there is inhibition, hesitation or reservation and seemingly a reluctance to witness God in such a dynamic and powerful way.

There may be many reasons for this, but partly it has to do with how we experience God and allow Him to fully affect our

---

[30] John 8:32.

lives with the truth that Jesus brings us and paid such a heavy price for, enabling us to accept, receive and grow into. It brings into question our growth in discipleship, and therefore how confident and secure we are in our walk of faith and willingness to share it with others.

It is what happens after our initial encounter with Jesus that is significant, when the 'honeymoon period' evaporates; where we find ourselves once more being pressed in by and swallowed up by the cares of the worldly life we lead, thus allowing God to slowly become an accessory to our lives rather than a necessity. We can easily fall back into a mindset that diminishes the enthusiasm we first had, at the same time intimidating us to comply with the attitude that our faith should be kept private. Nothing could be further from the truth.

Our relationship with God is not a quick fling of a romantic affair, but a lifelong and, in fact, eternal relationship. It does not stop when we stop feeling life is good. It does not stop when things are caving in around us. It does not stop when we feel a million miles from Him, or when the cares and concerns of our daily lives really are coming in on all sides, demanding our full attention.

He is not only present in all that life throws at us, good and bad, but is also Lord over it all. He reigns in all authority over everything. In all creation He has no equal, no competition. '"To whom then will you liken Me, Or *to whom* shall I be equal?" says the Holy One' (Isaiah 40:25). When we choose to follow Him, it is not a one-way encounter. To follow someone means you are with them and by default they are with you. Isn't that the case?

Grace is not an optional extra

If God is the instigator of our call to follow Him, then He not only takes the initiative, but is also the means through which our response is channelled. It is not possible for us through our own initiatives to direct the course of our relationship with Him without turning it into a formula that then breeds a religious spirit and institutionalises a framework of response: very sincere and full of good intention, but nonetheless far removed from the purpose God has for us in such a relationship.

Notice Jesus did not say, 'Come with me,' when He called those first disciples, but, 'Follow me.' Merely going along with someone does not necessarily commit you to their cause or intent. Following with the kind of commitment Jesus expects of us, I would suggest, requires an element of obedience and trust if we are to take seriously the commitment that is expected.

From our worldly perspective, I do not think we are able to understand, let alone embrace fully, the implications of such a sacrifice as dropping everything we know and are familiar with, and surrendering fully to Jesus by entrusting Him with our lives; completely, without necessarily knowing where He is taking us. So why trust what some might perceive as a foolhardy venture? After all, it is taking a huge leap of faith and responding to the vaguest and simplest of calls – just two words. Perhaps the answer lies not in what is said, but in who is saying it. I believe it is a trustworthy decision to make, because of what Jesus has already done for us. His track record speaks for itself. Everything about Him is centred on His grace.

Grace lies at the heart of what it means to be a follower of Jesus Christ. Our relationship with God is based on what He has done for us, not the other way round. It is God who took the initiative because He alone could bring us into that place of intimate relationship with Him in forgiveness and reconciliation. 'But God demonstrates His own love toward us, in that while we were still sinners, Christ died for us' (Romans 5:8).

This is what the cross on which Jesus was crucified is about – God reconciling humankind to Himself. We can add nothing to that. Nothing we attempt ourselves can accomplish what the sacrifice of Jesus accomplished. We cannot court favour with God through any means humanly possible, however sincere the 'good works' we strive to achieve are. We cannot justify ourselves before God in any other way than through His gracious intervention for us.

The only response we can validly make that is acceptable to God is to believe in His Son Jesus Christ and to follow His lead. He freely gave Himself for us so we might know eternal life through Him. This is grace – unmerited favour, undeserved blessing, and a gift. Paul explains it in this way:

> But God, who is rich in mercy, because of His great love with which He loved us, even when we were dead in trespasses, made us alive together with Christ (by grace you have been saved), and raised *us* up together … in the heavenly *places* in Christ Jesus … For by grace you have been saved through faith, and that not of yourselves; *it is* the gift of God, not of works, lest anyone should boast. For we are His workmanship, created in Christ Jesus for good works, which God prepared beforehand that we should walk in them.
> *Ephesians 2:4-10*

God has a planned purpose for our lives. He always has had, even before we were born; even before the world itself was created by Him.[31] We are 'His workmanship', as Paul explains. He is more than pleased with what He has created in us, but He has not finished with us yet.

Notice in this passage, we have been 'raised … up'. What does that imply? Through His grace upon our lives, we are called to reign with Him. This is what our calling is for. This is His purpose for our lives; that we should reign over the circumstances of where we have been placed, empowered to change the environment around us, not the other way round.

How many people are governed by their circumstances in life, whereby they feel disempowered rather than empowered in the everyday struggles they experience, without the ability to 'get on top of things'? Our mindset and world view must shift and,

---

[31] 2 Timothy 1:9.

since we are unable to accomplish that in our own strength, we are called to trust in the One who can change things in our lives and in us. But that requires transformation, a detoxing that moves us from a sinful or self-centred nature to an identity that embraces His love poured into us, reflecting His glory in us and through us. The world needs to see a radical difference demonstrated in us if it is to be convinced that this God is not only real and relevant, but also the 'Desire of All Nations' (Haggai 2:7).

Grace is not optional but essential if we are to fully grasp and understand the nature of our calling and implement it for the purpose God wants to fully release in us, with the effectiveness with which those first disciples had such an impact on the world around them.

Our human instinct is often, intrinsically set in our psyche, to seek out and settle for a way of following Jesus that makes little or no demand upon our lives. I sometimes wonder if we have settled for creating a church environment that has expectations that are too low, whereby we become consumerists in a weekly diet of fellowship with a programme-driven 'feed me' mentality that has little impact on us once we have left the church building to go our separate ways.

If that is so, then how, as His body, are we empowered to be released into our communities with a mission-minded determination to touch the lives of others with the gospel story that is alive in us?

Institutional religion devoid of a relationship with Jesus Christ is powerless to influence a world longing for a Saviour to be revealed and demonstrated. Jesus came demonstrating His message with signs and wonders, and with the full impact of heaven's resources wholly at His disposal. He called those early disciples to do likewise, and they did. He calls us to do likewise. His agenda has not changed. His mission has not changed. So what has, if we cannot see that same life-changing power released through us today? We have nothing to offer the world, no hope of salvation or transformation, if we are worldly in our discipleship and follow Jesus from an earthly rather than a kingdom perspective. Jesus never intended us to do that. Unless our discipleship is embedded in His grace, enabling us to be transformed by the renewing work of His Holy Spirit living in us, then our Christian walk becomes nothing more than a veneer, whereby underneath we remain living in the world with an earthly viewpoint, shaped and directed by all that we experience around us rather than by the One who is within us.

God has called us to be different, to be set apart,[32] which by its very nature has practical implications in our relationships and the way our discipleship directs us. We are constantly reminded that God's mission, and our part in it, is to permeate and transform our culture and society with the love that is God; the love in which and by which we are all created; the love that is in every human heart, however obscure it may appear.

If our following is to be meaningful and have an impact on those around us, it must embrace a relentless pursuit of the God who made Himself known and gave everything that we might experience and be changed by His love. We cannot and must not undermine the significance of that act of grace and the seriousness by which we are called to respond. It is too precious a gift for us to treat indifferently, superficially or callously.

Thought break

- How do you feel about God affecting you in a personal and intimate way through His Holy Spirit? What challenges or questions does this raise in you? What is your response?

- What does the word 'grace' imply in your relationship with God? What kind of grace do you live under?

- What significance do you think grace and mercy have in the mission of the Church? What role do they play in how we engage with and witness to our community?

---

[32] John 17:14, 1 Peter 1:16.

5

Staying Focused

I am a practical person. I like to get on and do, rather than talk about what needs doing. It is something that can frustrate Sheryl because she will at times suggest something that needs looking at and before she has finished her sentence, I'm up and doing it. I suspect I inherited that from my father. He was very practical with his hands and was forever engaged in getting on with various jobs, be it around the house or fixing things for other people. He was happiest when he was using his hands. He wasn't much of a conversationalist but would often sit and mull over solutions to practical problems that needed his attention. You could almost see the cog wheels turning in his head as he pondered and deliberated over the presenting issue. Then he would jump up and get to work, putting those thoughts into resolvable action. He could have several things on the go all at the same time. When he was successful, as often he was, he would sit down with a satisfied expression in his eyes. And then he would be thinking of the next task at hand. That was his nature.

    I am a lot like that at times. That does not mean I do not want to engage with people, but I naturally default to being active in getting on and getting things done. The trouble is, when I have my head in something, I am fully engrossed and often oblivious to anything else around me. I even lose track of time, absorbed in the task. That is fine to a point, but it can have disadvantages. Sometimes my focus can preclude others or even misdirect my attention from what is really needed. I can neglect other things that are perhaps more of a priority, and as a result cause upset, lost as I am in my own little world, however productive or justifiable the task may be.

Acting like this, we can often make assumptions, justifying our deeds with an attitude that we know what is best or we are confident in what we are doing. The trouble is that sometimes we do not get it right, and in the process of 'jumping in', without fully appreciating the real needs or perhaps being ill equipped for the task, what we push on with can become counterproductive and even damaging, especially to relationships.

That is particularly so when it comes to our discipleship. Following Jesus does not mean we have nothing to offer. But we can reduce our relationship with Him to 'doing' rather than 'being'. We can become engrossed in launching into something in our own strength or perception. We can be working in one place while God is at work somewhere else.

To be fully engaged with Him requires us to be obedient to His voice, His will and His direction and not be distracted by well-intentioned motives that misdirect our focus. We are not called to play guesswork with His will. He has given us the means to know and understand His purpose for us: 'But the Helper, the Holy Spirit, whom the Father will send in My name, He will teach you all things, and bring to your remembrance all things that I said to you' (John 14:26). I would suggest that the intimacy we embrace in God leaves little room for speculation. We have His Spirit living in us to make clear all things we are commissioned to walk in.

It is this intimacy that enables us to maintain our obedience to His voice. On one occasion, Jesus took three of his disciples – Peter, James and John – up a high mountain.[33] There they witnessed a transfiguration, whereby Jesus' whole appearance

---

[33] Matthew 17:1-8; Luke 9:28-36.

changed and was filled with light. From His face to His clothes, everything in Him radiated with incredible brilliance, as these bewildered disciples witnessed Him conversing with Moses and Elijah concerning all Jesus would face in Jerusalem and His ensuing departure. They would, I expect, have been filled with awe and terror, with all kinds of emotions running riot and the only response Peter could make was to do something practical. He suggested building three tabernacles to memorialise the event.

It is so normal for us to want to capture an event or experience that blows our mind, whether a spiritual encounter in a church gathering, or any other life-affecting event in our lives. We want to 'bottle it up' and preserve it. We want to re-enact the experience and revisit the emotions in some way, because of the impact it has had on us. We want to capture it on video or with photographs to share with others.

I suspect, if those three disciples had mobile phones with them, they would have requested a selfie with everyone present and sent it virally across the internet. But building tabernacles would have to suffice. However, their thinking was interrupted because they were missing an important point.

Why do you think Jesus took them up the mountain with Him in the first place? I have no doubt He knew what He was going there for and perhaps wanted them to share in the experience and expand their understanding of what His glory looked like. This was a divine encounter where heaven touched earth; a two-way interaction that revealed something very powerful and profound concerning the nature of who their master was and His purpose here on earth. This was an appointment that expressed the heart of God for His Son.

Interjecting before any monument could be erected, God gave them another directive. It was not just for them, but I believe for us too. 'While he [Peter] was speaking, behold, a bright cloud overshadowed them; and suddenly a voice came out of the cloud, saying, "This is My beloved Son, in whom I am well pleased. Hear Him!"' (Matthew 17:5). It is worth noting here that the NIV translates this as 'Listen to him!' We have 'hearing' and 'listening'. To hear, I would suggest, we need to listen. But we can listen without necessarily hearing. Someone can be talking to us and we give the appearance of listening, while at the same time being preoccupied with other thoughts. As a result, we are not fully taking in what they are saying. When we say to someone, 'I hear what you are saying,' we are acknowledging that we have taken on board all they have communicated.

To hear, we need to give our undivided attention when we are listening. It is something I am often at fault with, especially at home. I can be thinking about other things and miss the essence of what is being said, or I jump in midsentence, with the presumption of what the other person is going to say.

Listening to and hearing the person we are conversing with and seeing face to face is one thing. But it can be more challenging when we are conversing with God, whom we physically do not see. It is an area some struggle with when it comes to prayer, where we can often reduce the conversation to becoming one-sided; where we speak but do not listen, or even listen but do not hear. We can be distracted by all kinds of earthly sounds or thoughts that seek and often find our attention when we are trying to be still and listen.

Sitting in our garden once, as Sheryl and I sometimes do while spending time with God, we were conscious of the sound of the water pouring over the rocks in our pond. It is very calming and conducive to contemplative prayer. By contrast, noises in the background came into prominence: traffic passing by, a helicopter flying past and hovering overhead, the town hall clock chiming and various other sounds. We had to press in and focus, acknowledging the presence of these distractions and then dismissing them. We focused on the water and related it to Jesus' words describing streams of living water flowing through us, in John 7:38. The other sounds either stopped or became distant to our consciousness, and our ears became attentive once more to His voice.

Let the streams of His Spirit flow in you and underpin an inner sound that drowns out all other external noise. Cultivate an atmosphere of not just listening but also hearing. There is a delight in God's heart when we choose to spend time listening to His Son and hearing what He has to say to us. Spending valuable time in His presence can be more productive than busying ourselves with doing 'stuff'. There is a place for doing, but we also need to set aside time to be.[34]

Prayerful underpinning

If any relationship we enter is enhanced through healthy interaction and consistent participation through a two-way dialogue, then that must also apply to our relationship with God. But how can we nurture and develop such intimacy and keep it fresh and alive, without turning it into a routine-driven devotional obligation that feels dry and lifeless? I would suggest that without the Spirit's presence, we cannot truly engage with God on any level that involves intimacy. Any meaningful and deep-rooted interaction is built on the giving of ourselves to God, growing in discovering more about Him, understanding His will, searching His heart and placing our trust in Him. It is a desire to be with as well as to grow in knowledge of the One we choose to follow. To that end, prayer is central in engaging with, listening to and fostering a close-knit relationship, where we discover more about Him, more about ourselves and more about His purpose for our lives. Prayer should be the language of love we use when speaking of intimacy, rather than a ritualistically liturgical outpouring of words. It must engage the heart, not just the mind alone. It is a heart-to-heart encounter, or it is meaningless.

Jesus gives us clear direction of how that should apply to our prayer life: 'And when you pray, do not use vain repetitions as the heathen *do*. For they think that they will be heard for their

---

[34] Luke 10:38-42.

many words' (Matthew 6:7). It means finding the environment and creating the space that maximises our internal focus to fully engage with Him without distraction, whereby what is hidden from us becomes open and available; namely God's heart. For each of us, that 'room' (Matthew 6:6) we go into may be different, because we are each unique in our receptiveness. Our character, personality and experience will define what that will look like and where that may be.

Prayer is a primary means through which we relate to God, alongside engaging with and meditating on His word in Scripture. Three times Jesus mentions 'when you pray', not 'if' (Matthew 6:5-7). It is therefore a given that prayer is the norm for the disciple. It is not an option but a necessity. It is like breathing or eating and drinking; or at least, it should be. They are not 'ifs' in life but 'musts' to survive and be healthy. They are not things we dip into now and then when we feel like it. What would happen if you breathed or ate and drank with the same frequency as you prayed?

Prayer isn't a task we do, but a relationship we have. I don't speak to my wife because that's what spouses are supposed to do. We engage with one another because we are in a loving relationship and that naturally means we communicate through words, touch, gestures, gifts, etc; though I must admit, my communication isn't always what it ought to be. Similarly, prayer is vital to our spiritual health and well-being if we are to grow in our relationship with God. It is also essential to our emotional and physical well-being. It is a reminder that our lives are inseparable from the God who created us and made us in His image. He designed and fashioned us and knows our every need in life.

Many people find prayer difficult. Perhaps the dullness of routine is one reason some find it hard work and as such make it an infrequent 'dipping in' or when needs arise, rather than a natural part of their rhythm of life. Mere routine, repetition and familiarity in prayer can sometimes leave us feeling disengaged from God, making it mechanical or mundane. It is only through

Jesus that we can find that intimacy with the Father in prayer, empowered by His Spirit,[35] where such encounter brings us encouragement, motivation and purpose in that engagement.

So how did Jesus intend us to approach prayer? It is always as a child to a loving Father; as one whose whole dependency, security, direction, encouragement and trust rest upon the One who loves us and gave Himself for us. As Jesus points out, it is directed to God alone as expressed through the nearness of '*Abba*' or 'Daddy' (Romans 8:15). This makes it a conversation of intimacy, not formality; of openness and reliance, not distance and scepticism; of truthfulness and trust, not indifference and doubt. Our heavenly Father already knows what's on our hearts;[36] what our desires and hopes are; what makes us fearful or anxious; what our needs are and what we hide. He wants us to engage with Him openly and honestly.

It is an interesting thought that when we show interest in what is on His heart, He reciprocates by paying attention to what is on our heart. This is at the centre of how Jesus encourages us to pray. A dynamic and fulfilling prayer life depends on knowing that our Father understands our needs. It cuts to the chase.

The prayer that Jesus taught His disciples, as we read in Matthew 6:9-13, is perhaps the most important and significant means of embracing God from start to finish and channels our attention to who He is; reminding ourselves that He is God who is to be honoured, and His kingdom and His purpose are what He wants to establish in us; that He is God who meets our needs through His provision; that He is God whose forgiving Spirit enables us to focus on the gift of His mercy and forgiveness to encourage us to live in the place of being reconciled, and to impart it to others; that He is God whose protection empowers us to live as overcomers in a fallen world that wars with the concept of God's sovereign reign; and lastly, that He is God whose glory and power are eternally above all things.

---

[35] Romans 8:26-27.
[36] Matthew 6:8.

These are the aspects of following Him that we are to hold as our perspective and by which we align our lives and grow in knowledge and understanding of Him. These are the areas of our engagement with Him that can form the entirety of our prayer life but, however we unfold these focal points, we need to remind ourselves that this is not a one-way conversation directed at God, but rather shapes the nature of the interaction He has with us as well as we with Him. That, in its emphasis, will vary, because at different times different aspects of this prayer will have greater relevance to us, and His Spirit may lead us to spend longer focusing on the areas He wants more specifically to draw our attention to.

We may need to be reminded of His sovereignty and greatness because of difficult circumstances we find ourselves in, perhaps even encountering and experiencing persecution and hostility directed at our faith.

We may need to cooperate with His kingdom advancement in our engagement with His mission and outreach as we step out and require heaven's presence to be released into those areas and people we seek to influence with the gospel.

We may need to lean into Him for provision in times of need or difficulty, knowing with confidence that daily He provides for us and that He is the 'bread of life' (John 6:35).

We may find ourselves struggling with issues of unforgiveness and need to be reminded that we live in a place of reconciliation with God who has forgiven us, and that carries the responsibility that we too must be merciful and gracious in forgiving others.

We may need to be reminded that we have a loving Father in heaven who deeply cares for us, and that may be pertinent if we are struggling with our identity and lack confidence in who we are or are fearful of the evil around us.

We may need to remind ourselves that He is sovereign over all things and has no equal, whereby He reigns far above all things and holds all things in His hand.

This is therefore not a single or solitary prayer to be merely recited, but the way in which we engage heart to heart with the One who directs and guides our lives and with whom we are in intimate relationship. It is here that we need to cultivate a rhythm of life that incorporates encounter that is relevant and meaningful to our everyday experiences of life. It is this rhythm of life that includes and is affected by spending quality time with God. I would suggest it is a necessity rather than an option. Jesus found it vital to get away regularly and spend time alone with His Father in 'solitary' places away from the crowds and distractions (Luke 5:16). If He needed to operate from this place of intimacy, how much more do we?

Persistence that pays

How would you describe your staying power? How easily do you give up when things don't appear to go as you expected, or when prayers seem unanswered? We live in a world that wants quick answers and fast resolutions. We want things to happen yesterday. Our mindset in such an environment is conditioned to adopt a spirit of intolerance and impatience and to give up as soon as we don't get the results we want.

Jesus gives us a different perspective when it comes to prayer. 'Ask, and it will be given to you; seek, and you will find; knock, and it will be opened to you. For everyone who asks receives, and he who seeks finds, and to him who knocks it will be opened' (Matthew 7:7-8). Jesus deals here with our persistence and perseverance in prayer and challenges our perception of who God is as Father. We know how to give good things rather than bad to those we love. How much more should we trust God to do likewise; and more so.[37]

The two issues are tied together because they deal with our relationship with Him, our trust in Him and our understanding of His goodness to us as the perfect Father. Nothing exposes our maturity as disciples more than our commitment to prayer,

---

[37] Matthew 7:9-12.

which more than anything reveals how either deep-rooted or shallow we are in Him.

Jesus' desire is that we grow in maturity in Him. He wants our ministry to prosper; our mission to be successful. He has called us to bear fruit.[38] But He has also called us to walk in the power of His Spirit with confidence and authority. That is our inheritance. He wants to release everything in us and through us that is of His kingdom. That requires a total reliance and dependency on Him through a prayer-filled walk of faith that grows with every step. We would not entrust a two-year-old child with a responsibility that only an older child would have the capacity to handle. Similarly, God wants to entrust us with so much more, but we need the capacity to handle it responsibly. If we remain shallow in our faith, we never grow to that level of trust with the things He wants to release in us.

Immaturity can also cause us to become complacent or flippant. Think of a spoilt child who gets everything they want at the click of their fingers or stamping of their feet in tantrum. How is that child's character shaped and formed? How mature and stable will they grow to become?

Jesus is refining and shaping us and releasing us in the fullness of responsibility as His witnesses. He will not give us anything that will harm or jeopardise His plans and purposes for us. The furtherance of His kingdom is advanced by the follower whose walk with God is so close, 'no' is not an option, because they already know God's heart and press in to obtain that which has already been expressed in heaven.

The key to this level of growth in our prayer life lies in these three words Jesus uses: 'ask', 'seek' and 'knock'. These are three verbs, and each has a different emphasis, implying that we have a variety of ways to act upon and interact with, using multiple senses. It carries with it a confidence that we are engaging with God, and He hears our prayer and will answer accordingly. These three areas combined involve prayer in the whole of our

---

[38] John 15:1-8.

being. Let's look at each in turn to discover their emphasis.

The first, 'ask', is verbal. This is about engaging with God in conversational dialogue, communicating with Him. Apart from Jesus, one of the most significant people in Scripture who dialogued with God was Moses. He had an intimate conversation with God on many occasions, moment by moment. And Moses would argue his case on behalf of God's people, persuading, challenging, pleading and even 'changing' God's mind.[39] Jesus is encouraging us to have this same attitude in our communication with Him. We are called to engage with and wrestle with God in dialogue; not as a shopping list approach but in deep, meaningful conversation that has impact. '"Let us reason together," Says the LORD' (Isaiah 1:18). We are called to walk with Him, moment by moment, every day of our lives, in conversation with Him. Ask and keep on asking, because the promise here is that it will be given to us. The question, perhaps, is how serious we are in wanting it. God has called us into a relationship with Him that requires our response to His will; our engaging with Him to release what He has purposed, so heaven's resources can flood our earthly circumstances. How often do we 'not receive' because we do not ask or because we do so with the wrong motives (James 4:2-3)?

The second verb Jesus uses, 'seek', is visual. This involves a different part of our senses. Visual is about seeing and seeing is perceiving. It's seeing the bigger picture. It's saying to God, 'Show me what You are doing; show me what this is about; where this is going; Your plans and purposes for me/us.' It's a chasing after God, to see what He is doing and recognise what He is calling us to. It is not enough to ask and sit back passively for something to fall into our lap. We must actively seek it out, pressing into God, alert in anticipation and expectation; all the time looking for signs and promptings and hints. He wants us to see with His eyes, and that's why He draws our attention to

---

[39] Exodus 32:9-14; 33:11,13-17.

visual things: visions, pictures, events unfolding, dreams and anything that will visually grab our attention. Time and again we see in the Old Testament God asking the prophets, 'What do you see?' (for example, Jeremiah 1:11,13) or giving them visual perceptions and visions of things He is unfolding, such as Ezekiel 1:4 and 10:1. Similarly, God is inviting us with the same question: 'What do you see? What is it you are looking out for?'

Jesus only did what He saw His Father doing, as He asserted in John 5:19, and here we are encouraged to adopt the same stance; to see what Father is doing and work alongside, as Jesus did. It is here in the prophetic area of prayer that God often reveals things to us, bringing us insight into what He wants to do or release to us. But the fact that God has brought us revelation does not in itself mean that it is an automatic given. We are called to actively release it through our declaration, that we are in agreement with His will and intent.

The third verb, 'knock', I describe as physical. God wants us to be 'forceful' in prayer. By that, I don't mean destructive or reckless, but passionate to the point of distraction. We would normally knock on a door that is shut to us and we want entry to. A doorway takes us from one reality to another (for example, from one room to another, or from outside to inside). Jesus encourages us to bang on that door until something happens. It's not a gentle tap and then walking away if nothing happens or no one answers. It's more like a police raid where the officers hammer on the door, shouting, 'Open up!'

God wants you and me to be pressing into His kingdom and not giving up until we see breakthrough in a situation where we need to see heaven invade earth. It's a crying out from the depth of our hearts, relentlessly pressing in. Time and again Jesus gave us parables portraying this. The man calling at midnight, banging on the door of his friend, asking for bread, in Luke 11:5-8. The persistent widow demanding justice from the judge, in Luke 18:1-8. The woman pleading for her demon possessed-daughter to be set free, in Matthew 15:21-28. The centurion who crossed his cultural divide to plead his case for his sick servant, in Luke 7:1-10. All those who came looking, came banging on His door. God wants us to be persistent and asks the question, 'How serious are you about this; how much do you want this?' How much you want God's outpouring presence in your life, your church, your community is based on how committed you are to relentlessly pursue that breakthrough. It's about not giving up until we see that release, that breaking-in of His kingdom and His promise into our situation.

When we ask and don't get, do we then give up, or suppose God hasn't heard? Do we maybe come back to it half-heartedly and intermittently, not expecting much? Discipleship cannot be half-hearted or fickle if we are to effectively follow Him and do all He has commissioned us to do. Intimacy is at the heart of our calling because it is from this that everything else flows.

When Jesus calls us to ask, seek and knock, He means keep on doing it; don't stop. Persistence isn't about tantrum throwing in a supermarket, stamping our feet until we get what we want, or embarrassing our parents enough for them to relent. That is immaturity. To keep asking and seeking God and banging on His door is to take seriously the things He has put on our hearts, the things that He wants to release to us and through us. The power of the Holy Spirit living in us is not a genie in a lamp resource to be conjured up, but a relationship with the living God. He is not there at our bidding, but we, as His disciples, are at His.

Persistence is character forming, but, more than that, it is a necessary weapon in the spiritual battles we face every day that would seek to deflate us, cause us to doubt and render us powerless. Prayer is a weapon that destroys enemy strongholds, levels mountains, sends the enemy running, changes the environment.

Our battle is against the one who comes to 'steal, and to kill, and to destroy' (John 10:10). The one thing that causes Satan to shudder is our intimacy with God through a mature prayer life. If Satan is petitioning God, asking for permission to create carnage,[40] and the Church (ie you and me) is not engaging Him with the same intensity through prayer for His will to be released, is God then not restricted in the outcome? He wants to hear us because He wants to answer us.

God not only answers prayers, but He also answers them well. It is His nature to give us 'good gifts' (Matthew 7:11); or as Luke's version terms it, in Luke 11:13, the gift of His Spirit, from whom all good things flow. When God's answer is 'no', it's because He has a better 'yes' for us further down the line than the 'yes' we're asking for now.[41] He wants to shower us with the resources of heaven, His reality coming into ours. He chooses to do that most effectively when we engage with Him.

Fasting is not an option

When Jesus and the three disciples returned from the mountain, they were confronted with a disruptive situation. A crowd had gathered around an incident. From their midst, a father came running to Jesus and, throwing himself down on his knees before Him, pleaded with despair: 'Lord, have mercy on my son, for he is an epileptic and suffers severely; for he often falls into the fire and often into the water. So I brought him to Your disciples, but they could not cure him' (Matthew 17:15-16).

Often, we can pray for someone to be healed and nothing or little appears to happen. Sometimes, we press in and over time healing takes place, either supernaturally or through medical intervention. Both, I would say, are miraculous. But Jesus' response suggests an expectation that should have brought results: 'Then Jesus answered and said, "O faithless and perverse generation, how long shall I be with you? How long shall I bear with you? Bring him here to Me"' (Matthew 17:17). They brought the child to Jesus, who cast the demon out, bringing healing there and then.

I would imagine the disciples, who were expected to do what

---

[40] Job 1:6-12; Luke 22:31-32.
[41] Isaiah 55:8-9.

Jesus did but failed to, may have felt somewhat sheepish and embarrassed. Even in Jesus' day, there would have been an anticipation that His disciples would minister with the same authority and power as He did. That surely was also Jesus' expectation, for He commissioned them to do as He did: healing the sick, casting out demons, raising the dead and proclaiming the gospel – and more besides.[42] Was He therefore aiming those critical comments at His disciples or the wider crowd? The disciples were certainly implicated, because when they questioned Him as to why they could not do what He just did, He made that abundantly clear:

> So Jesus said to them, 'Because of your unbelief; for assuredly, I say to you, if you have faith as a mustard seed, you will say to this mountain, "Move from here to there," and it will move; and nothing will be impossible for you. However, this kind does not go out except by prayer and fasting.'
> *Matthew 17:20-21*

How much importance we place on prayer and fasting depends on how we view this area of our walk with God and what its purpose is. Jesus said, as we noted with prayer, 'when you fast', not 'if you fast' (Matthew 6:16). Here He draws our attention to a hypocritical aspect or approach to fasting: that of bringing attention to ourselves and making a song and dance of it in the process.

Prayer and fasting go hand in hand, drawing everything within us to a place of focus and surrender, where our physical self aligns with our spirit to fully enhance our commitment to the One we are praying to. The space given by that self-denial, that act of going without, needs to be used as a springboard towards the intimacy we enter and not, as in the case of abstinence from food, spending time thinking about when we can next eat. Fasting has a purpose, a goal, which we choose to

---

[42] See, for example, Matthew 10:6-8; Luke 10:9.

engage with from the start.

Jesus pointed out to His disciples that for them to have succeeded where they had failed would have required a deeper preparation, whereby fasting alongside prayer would have equipped them better for the task. Was there an expectation, therefore, that His disciples should have stopped, fasted and prayed and then ministered to the child? Did Jesus fast and pray before coming back down the mountain and tackling the issue? The question is somewhat superfluous, because I believe the prayer and fasting Jesus is referring to here is one of preparedness and therefore an ongoing engagement involving both.

Fasting in a prayerful context and environment is something that takes place inside us, not just externally. It is primarily about drawing into the heart of God and therefore being in the right place relationally to respond to situations and circumstances from an inner core of intimacy that translates into exercised authority, because it is released from a place of compassion and love for those in need. It is not a random means by which we execute some form of emergency ministry, but a lifestyle that acts as a reservoir of His grace and presence within us, drawing upon the resources of heaven to implement the purposes of God for the benefit of others. I believe it is an area that is often misunderstood and even misused within the Church, as a random 'get out of jail' response to a crisis. Even in the context of an annual Lenten fast, as part of the Church's liturgical calendar, how seriously do we take the reason for engaging with this requirement? In some cases, it can become a focus on what we are fasting from, at a minimal level of discomfort, thus making it in attitude like that of making new year's resolutions. But to what effect?

To understand what Jesus was getting at, we have a more comprehensive description in Isaiah 58:1-7 of how not to fast. Israel worshipped and sacrificed with regularity and zeal, but their approach was in the spirit of religion and was not worked through in their attitude towards others, particularly regarding justice and fairness. Real needs of the people were ignored and even abused, and Israel could not understand or comprehend why God had closed His ears to their supplications and prayers. Their fasting in effect counted for nothing and had probably as much impact as trying to start a car with a flat battery – it went nowhere. Here God spells out the purpose of fasting, fervently unpacking its nature. It is not only pleasing to Him but underlines the reasons for doing it.

> *Is* this not the fast that I have chosen:
> To loose the bonds of wickedness,
> To undo the heavy burdens,
> To let the oppressed go free,
> And that you break every yoke?
> *Is it* not to share your bread with the hungry,
> And that you bring to your house the poor who are cast out;
> When you see the naked, that you cover him.
> And not hide yourself from your own flesh?
> *Isaiah 58:6-7*

Fasting is therefore a response to need; not our own, but that of others. God was the first to respond to the need of humankind when He saw the injustice and inhumanity that our own brokenness and sin had caused, and in His compassion He sent His own Son, Jesus, to address and deal with it once and for all upon the cross. The first thing Jesus did at the start of His ministry was to declare His intentions: 'The Spirit of the Lord *is* upon Me, Because He has anointed Me' to respond (Luke 4:18-19). Responding to human need is central to fasting with purpose. It is saying, 'I will not sit comfortably or rest easy while others are suffering.' This is the call of the disciple. Jesus' response is our response. We are sent by Jesus in the same way His Father sent Him.[43]

If we are to be about our Father's business in this way, it

---

[43] John 20:21.

requires us to engage in His mission from a place of being with Him first. This is the springboard that takes us into a broken world. Rich Villodas writes 'any talk of being engaged in the world must begin not with activity but with a life in God'.[44]

Fasting in this context becomes a wrestling with God, taking us out of our comfort zone. It is not a 'hunger strike' but an equipping. It is not about deprivation but enrichment. Fasting, like prayer, needs our regular and consistent attention to enable us to be in tune with God's purposes for us on a moment-by-moment basis. What we are released into is underpinned by the amount of quality time we spend with Him. It enables us to meet and address needs as and when they arise, from a place of intimacy, because it focuses us to what we are called to, bringing heaven on earth. Regular fasting stores up the spiritual sensitivity in us like a reservoir, from which we can access that which God desires for us to be released to others.

Let's remind ourselves that God created us to be community. A healthy community consists of key fundamental elements. It involves embracing and being a caring society that meets needs among all. It includes family welfare that enriches and brings prosperity. It acts as the correction of human behaviour that is deviant or gone astray. It takes seriously the need for restoration and continuity that strengthens our social fabric. It takes responsibility for the well-being of all members, where there is blessing and all are valued and honoured.

This kind of fasting is not fruitless. Nor is it taking 'pot shots in the dark', hoping that somehow God may respond positively. It carries the promise of reward. When we approach prayer and fasting in this manner on a consistent basis, heaven responds.

When we fast, then we see things happen. Light breaks out in the darkness; healing springs up; His righteousness and glory go before us and watch our back; He answers when we call; He guides us continually; He provides for us; He strengthens us; we become like a spring where waters never fail to flow; He brings

---

[44] Rich Villodas, *The Deeply Formed Life* (Colorado Springs: Waterbrook Press, 2020), p170.

fruitfulness.[45]

If by fasting we are enhancing our discernment in seeking God's heart and will for us as His followers, then discovering His purpose and seeing that when it is released in our ministry, it carries with it the blessing of success; even restoring in our communities that which may have been lost or broken for generations. God does everything well.[46]

We have all experienced how good it feels when we have blessed someone with a gift or an act of service and seen the joy on their face. God wants to bless us in His service. The regularity of our prayer and fasting matures us in our relationship with Him.

Unless we take seriously what intimacy with Jesus involves in terms of our commitment to Him, our discipleship will always fall short of the potential and possibilities He wants us to walk in and release into our community and environment. It is here that the focus of our attention needs to be streamed. It is compassion that we respond to. The compassion of God laid bare in our hearts, calling for our response to His love, whereby our attention in prayer becomes a single cry that we may align our hearts and will to His and be moved to respond with the same compassion stirring in us. It is here that the reservoirs of our fasting unleash the powers of heaven to saturate the earth, releasing healing, restoration, reconciliation, forgiveness, repentance or whatever else is tugging at the Father's heartstrings that He then calls us to administer.

---

[45] Isaiah 58:8-12.
[46] Isaiah 55:8-11.

Thought break

- How easy or difficult do you find prayer? What are the things that make it so? What would you describe your priorities to be when praying to God?

- How would you describe the rhythm of your life and the place of persistent prayer in it, and how healthy do you consider that to be? What areas do you need to develop when it comes to asking, seeking and knocking, as described in this chapter?

- Fasting is about spending time reflecting and understanding what God is calling you to. What are God's priorities for your life? How do you know or discover what they are? What is your pattern or commitment to regular fasting? How full is your reservoir?

Part 2
The Nature of Following

6

Capacity to Grow

Transformation concerns the nature of who we are and who we become. It is not emulating who Jesus is, but rather being embraced and captivated by His presence, whereby our nature becomes entwined with His nature to such a degree that His desire becomes our desire, His compassion becomes our compassion, His purpose becomes our purpose and His heart becomes our heart. This is what I believe being like Him incorporates.

Is it not here that Jesus becomes more visible in us? Is it not here where our intimacy with Him ultimately lies? Is it not here that we take on His nature and are transformed by the work of His Holy Spirit living in us, so that our identity is firmly anchored in the God who came to claim and restore us? This is who He created us to be. He came to save us not just *from* something, but *for* something.

Sheryl and I love decorating and improving our home. When you own a house, there is always ongoing maintenance to be getting on with and improvements to be made. In the various houses we have lived in, putting our own stamp on them has always motivated and excited us and we have made it one of our priorities whenever we move to a new home.

Sheryl does not particularly relish the mess of stripping away old décor, or engaging in repairs that mean taking out before putting back, with all the disorder that ensues, but we both know it is an important part of the process of renewing and transforming our home, structurally as well as aesthetically. Discovering what 'horrors' lie underneath is unnerving but also rewarding because it enables us to put right and repair whatever is needed, with the satisfaction of knowing things are as they should be with no hidden surprises.

I believe it is a similar scenario when God undertakes to transform us. There are things in our lives that need sorting. Things that are not healthy and can be hidden out of sight, even for many years, masked by a veneer or 'décor' that gives the appearance everything is fine in our lives; at least, to those looking in from the outside. But left undealt with, they can become a stumbling block to any move God wants to lead us forward in. These things can become barriers that prevent us from fully knowing the peace, joy, hope and love that He wants us not only to experience, but also to live under. It is here that being released into a place of freedom truly enables us to be empowered and equipped with everything He wants to give us.

Transformation is not simply an aesthetic improvement or a quick makeover. It is a renovation. It may be the 'same house', but restored; it has changed dramatically, being more solid, secure and inviting. It is a change in every sense of the word. We become a 'new creation', with a new identity, yet still maintain who we uniquely are created to be, but with old things that are unhelpful passing away (2 Corinthians 5:17). We no longer live under condemnation, haunted by guilt, fear, shame, unworthiness or any other accusations that pull us down.[47] Such a work of God in us is a process; one in which we cooperate with His Spirit to bring about.

Since moving into our current Victorian house a few years ago, we have done much to improve it. Regarding decorating, we reached the stage of doing the hallway, having completed all the rooms. We set about stripping the heavy embossed paper from the ceilings upstairs and downstairs. You are never quite

---

[47] Romans 8:1.

sure what such paper hides or supports, and why it was necessary to cover the lathe and plaster ceilings in the first place. Upstairs was fine; downstairs a little less so. There were some long cracks, but it all seemed to be holding well. Our thinking was to engage a plasterer to just skim over the surface and that would be fine. But when he arrived and inspected the state of the ceiling, he made it abundantly clear that the old plaster needed to be taken down and a new ceiling erected. It was too dangerous to remain. It was clear our decision was made for us.

Sometimes we can convince ourselves that the state of things is not as bad as we might think; that somehow, we can get by or get away with things and it will be alright. We can fail to realise hidden dangers or problems further down the line. That applies to our lives as well as our dwelling places.

God knows us better than we know ourselves. He knows where and how to focus His transforming love towards us and where we need to be healed, set free, reassured and loved. He does not pay us quick visits but indwells us, so that His transforming work in our lives is ongoing. When we choose to follow Jesus, there is purpose in it.

Following His resurrection, when Jesus appeared to those anxious disciples huddled together in hiding, He did two things. He reassured them of His peace and that it was really Him, and He commissioned them with the same assignment He had been given by His Father. There was a lot for them to comprehend, not least His sudden and unexpected appearance.

> When He had said this, He showed them *His* hands and His side. Then the disciples were glad when they saw the Lord.
> So Jesus said to them again, 'Peace to you! As the Father has sent Me, I also send you.' And when He had said this, He breathed on *them*, and said to them, 'Receive the Holy Spirit. If you forgive the sins of any, they are forgiven them; if you retain the *sins* of any, they are retained.'
> *John 20:20-23*

Sometimes our change of circumstances creates uncertainty, doubt or anxiety in us as we adjust to things that are unfamiliar or unexpected. Change inevitably is unsettling at the best of times, but more so when it takes us out of our known environment and into an unpredicted setting, where we struggle to get our heads around what is going on, or perhaps not going on.

It is here we need to be assured by His peace, to settle our minds to accommodate such encounters and process the rationale, so we can adjust our perspective. What Jesus had to say to these disciples was so significant, they needed to really understand what He was handing on to them. And so do we. They would be released with the same assignment Jesus had been sent with. Not only that, but they were also expected to carry that assignment out in the same way, empowered by the same Holy Spirit as He was.

It was important they did not go charging ahead in their own strengths and abilities, however enthusiastic and passionate about this mission they may have become. 'Behold, I send the Promise of My Father upon you; but tarry in the city of Jerusalem until you are endued with power from on high' (Luke 24:49). They had to wait.

Jesus often takes us to unfamiliar places and situations that require us to rely on Him and lean into Him. Consider this. Those first disciples spent three years following Him, learning from Him, growing close to Him. They saw and experienced so much of what He did, and yet they still had to wait. It was not passive waiting, but participating and engaging with the Holy Spirit, which enabled active waiting. In that time, they grew in spiritual capacity as they stayed and prayed together, so by the time they were filled with the Holy Spirit, they were able to receive the fullness of all that God would pour into them.

There are no shortcuts in our relationship with Jesus if we are to be effective and fruitful in the things that He calls us to accomplish. There must therefore be a mind shift and a radical turnaround in our nature, because our natural response is to engage with an earthly capacity and perspective rather than a kingdom-centred one.

The capacity of expansion

When we read through the Gospel accounts, we see that the disciples, while witnessing to and participating in Jesus' ministry, were bewildered, confused, uncertain and playing catch-up a lot of the time.

We too live with the tension of having an experiential faith in an amazing God who can do all things and for whom nothing is impossible, and at the same time feeling vulnerable, inadequate and ill-equipped for the tasks we are often called to participate in. It goes with the territory, because we are limited when left to our human resources alone. If it were not so, we would not need the empowering presence of God's Holy Spirit. Nor would we need to walk in intimacy with Him to accomplish things. But our discipleship is such that our reliance on Him is crucial.

Our ability to successfully engage with His mission is determined by the capacity in us to contain His presence. There is only so much we can hold in our minds at any one time. There is a limit to how much we can comprehend the things of God that are well beyond our jurisdiction. Jesus understood that and it is why He made clear to His disciples the need for them to wait, to be filled and empowered:

> I still have many things to say to you, but you cannot bear *them* now. However, when He, the Spirit of truth, has come, He will guide you into all truth; for He will not speak on His own *authority*, but whatever He hears He will speak; and He will tell you things to come.
> *John 16:12-13*

We cannot expand our understanding or experience of God without His Spirit opening our eyes and hearts to comprehend Him and take in all that this relationship involves. Our limited knowledge of God needs to increase, so we may know Him more and grow in the fullness of His presence in us. My experience is that this is often realised in line with the areas in which we engage with Him and the people to whom He draws us to minister.

Our capacity to host more of His presence is necessary to release His divine will into our lives with effectiveness, whether that is showing an act of kindness to someone, pronouncing healing on a sick person or raising someone from the dead. We may or may not be called to encounter and release the latter, but we are expected to love others in all the practicalities of our everyday relationships with the people we meet and share our lives with.

In that respect, capacity is increased by the measure of compassion our hearts are filled with. How hungry are we to see more of Him fill more of us with His heart? That may not always be straightforward. It involves more than simply desiring it. There is a practical implication we must understand and consider.

If you think about the contents of a kettle or jug filled with water, and try to pour the entire volume of that water into a single cup, what will happen? Clearly it will overflow once it has reached the cup's limit and the rest of the water will be spilt onto the floor and lost. More is wasted than caught because the capacity of one is greater than the other; no matter how hard you try, the latter cannot contain the former. And yet, when it comes to our relationship with God, we can at times have unrealistic expectations of His working in our lives and, as a result, experience disappointment or frustration when things do not turn out as we sometimes pray they might. Paul encourages us 'to know the love of Christ which passes knowledge; that you may be filled with all the fullness of God' (Ephesians 3:19). To be released by Him, we need to be immersed in Him.

Our relationship with God is not static, like the cup with fixed capacity. It is ongoing and grows. I would liken it more to a potter throwing a vessel. As He works the clay on the wheel, the potter's skilful hands enable the form to expand and rise to the capacity the potter intends it to contain. We are an ongoing work in progress. God continually fills us to the fullness of the measure we can contain. But His desire is that we increase and grow in maturity, so He can pour even more of Himself into our lives as our capacity to host Him enlarges.

As we grow in our commitment to Him, so He goes on filling us with more of Himself. It is an ongoing process. It never runs out. We will never be able to contain everything that is God, because He is greater and far beyond anything in His entire creation. But we can be filled with all His love for us, and it is this love that we hold and release to others. It is in this love that we can expand and grow, thus containing and releasing more and more of His mercy, His grace and His peace.

As our capacity is enlarged, so is our ability to engage effectively in the areas into which He calls us to release His presence and power. What may have felt difficult and alien becomes increasingly second nature as we continue to live from that place of relationship with Him.

The first time I prayed for someone to be healed, I was steeped in uncertainty, awkwardness and a degree of scepticism. As my relationship with Jesus grew, so I was able to pray and minister from a place of greater anticipation and expectation, and over the years have witnessed some remarkable and unforgettable healings, as well as experiencing personal ones.

Being faithful to the things God entrusts us with opens more possibilities as we continue to follow Him and allow Him to move in our lives. He wants to enlarge our influence and effectiveness as His disciples and release us into the fullness of His purposes. 'For to everyone who has, more will be given, and he will have abundance; but from him who does not have, even what he has will be taken away' (Matthew 25:29). Our greatest prayer then surely becomes, 'More, Lord. Whatever You want to do, I say "yes". I just want more of You; more of Your presence in my life, that You may be glorified in me with ever-increasing measure.'

The capacity of perception

How we perceive things affects how we respond to them. So what happens when the life you thought you were living suddenly changes and your perspective needs to radically shift? What if, in addition, you find yourself at odds with your previously held sound and secure world view, which is now making you feel increasingly uncomfortable?

Part of the transformation process in our discipleship heightens our awareness of our prejudices and taboos. God has a habit of challenging our perception to align it with His. But that can be an uncomfortable and even painful process because it causes us to rethink our previously held attitudes, some of which may need to be ditched to accommodate the thought process God wants us to adopt and become our new reality.

Even as mature Christians, we can harbour negative attitudes and responses towards others whose lifestyle we do not condone, or find uncomfortable, for a whole number of reasons. Such prejudicial limitations make it difficult to engage with the very people God wants us to reach out to, or build relationships with. As a result, we can dismiss opportunities to touch people's lives.

Peter found himself in such a dilemma. He had spent time with Jesus, witnessing to the compassionate love that was practically demonstrated to all manner of people, and yet there was still the human side to Peter that exposed His prejudicial vulnerability.

It would have been Peter's customary practice to pray at various times in the day, and it was no exception when at midday he went up to the housetop to do just that, in the place where he was lodging by the sea – a house owned by Simon the tanner. Nothing out of the ordinary, not even when he became very hungry, and while a meal was being prepared, 'he fell into a trance' (Acts 10:10). The vision Peter then saw may well have been stimulated by his empty stomach. Either way, God was guiding his thoughts in another direction, addressing a prejudicial mindset that needed to be altered for what God was putting Peter's way. He was shown food lowered down from heaven, with an invitation to take and eat. The problem was the sheet displayed all kinds of creatures that Peter knew to be unclean and common. It went against everything he believed to be true. He did not want to contaminate himself because the Law of God forbade it and, as a Jew, he would have been screaming abhorrence at the very thought of such a suggestion.

We all carry or hold certain preconceived ideas that are culturally defined or experientially perceived, sometimes through external influences. They can hide our inner detrimental thoughts even from our conscious selves until circumstances force them to the surface.

> But Peter said, 'Not so, Lord! For I have never eaten anything common or unclean.'
> And a voice *spoke* to him again the second time, 'What God has cleansed you must not call common.'
> Acts 10:14-15

It was clearly a disturbed wrestling that Peter was undergoing, because God had to repeat it three times for His intentions to sink in. Unbeknown to Peter, God was already paving the way for an encounter He was directing Peter's way with a Roman centurion named Cornelius. Bear in mind this was a taboo subject. It was a no-go area when it came to Jews communicating or mixing with non-Jews, let alone those of occupying forces.

When God is putting things our way, He calls us to engage with Him first, to release His heart, His purpose into our path. He has already gone on ahead of us to prepare the way and bring His presence into the situation He sends us into. Rich Villodas states: 'Long before we act, God has already acted. Long before we speak, God has already spoken. Long before we arrive, God has been present.'[48] We are called to recognise and respond to

---

[48] Villodas, *The Deeply Formed Life*, p181.

what He has already set in motion. It is our preparedness or not that determines the outcome.

God had already arranged what for Peter was an unforeseen meeting with clear intent. Messengers were on their way to Simon's house as God confirmed His purpose to Peter, so the connection could be made:

> While Peter thought about the vision, the Spirit said to him, 'Behold, three men are seeking you. Arise therefore, go down and go with them, doubting nothing; for I have sent them.'
> *Acts 10:19-20*

There are times when God needs to increase our capacity to fully perceive His intentions in the situations and encounters that He calls us to engage with, which may be contrary to our willingness to do so. The fact that He goes on ahead of us, putting in place the conditions for His purposes to be released, should encourage us that He has intentioned what lies ahead, plans that He requires us to step into. But He also knows that we need to be convinced that they are His will for us, and so the obstacles in our way need to be addressed; namely, our own perception of what we are called to embark on.

The challenge Peter underwent is a familiar one when God wants our attention to address an issue with which He confronts us. Conviction is necessary to fully engage with what we are being called to. Coercion is never a good way forward. God doesn't want to coerce us, but rather to convict us to participate with Him in what He is doing.

For that, we need to continually engage with Him, so our thoughts are aligned with His. It is from a place of intimacy that we can fully discern that perfect will and willingly step into its path, even where previously there may have been reluctance on our part to do so. God is never in a hurry, but does want our full attention and compliance.

From personal encounter (v10), God then endorses and confirms His purpose (v20), and then brings conviction for us to engage with His plans fully according to His will (v28). When our natural disposition becomes that of anticipation and expectation, it is astonishing what emerges from our encounter with God and what is released. We have been entrusted with a mission that carries with it His approval. It means we have an empowered mandate to engage with.

> To be entrusted with the gospel of truth means that God trusts us with it. It is precious, as are the people who need to receive it. He will only trust us with it if He knows we will not misuse it, neglect it or abuse it. Why? Because His name and His reputation are at stake, not ours. Therefore, He will only entrust it to those who have surrendered all to Him and live for Him, because His Word carries the power to transform lives, to open blind eyes, to heal the sick and to release people from all kinds of bondage and oppressions.[49]

The need for our cooperation is interwoven with His directing our lives in a transformational process that refines our thinking and our attitude and leads us to be more openly accepting of the opportunities to share His compassionate love with those He is leading us to.

What then becomes possible is limitless, as it was in Peter's case. Not only did Cornelius, his family and all those he invited to hear Peter's message believe and surrender their lives to God, but they were also filled with the Holy Spirit, and presumably from there started out on their own discipleship journey with Jesus.

That is the power the gospel of Jesus holds, one we have been called to share and demonstrate in the fullness of all that God wants to accomplish through it. We should not limit what that might mean for us, both as individual believers and as a Church in mission.

If God has given us the blueprints to build a Porsche, we

---

[49] Pradella, *I AM Relational*, p152.

should not settle for building a go-cart. Our walk with Him by its nature should continually increase our capacity for His Holy Spirit to live more fully in us and be released with greater impact and influence through us.

Thought break

- How 'equipped' do you feel as a follower of Jesus? How hungry are you to grow deeper in Him?

- How would you describe God's investment in you? In what way would someone else notice any changes or growth in your walk of faith?

- What shapes your prejudices? How valid or justifiable do you think they are? How do you respond when God challenges those presuppositions and prompts you to confront and address them?

7

Positioned for Purpose

It can sometimes be the case that opportunities to participate in ministry or mission in the community do not immediately present themselves in the normal course of our busy lives and can therefore remain untapped and dormant. Sometimes it requires boldness or vision to spark a flame and start a fire that impassions and ignites a move of God in our midst, drawing us towards something we would never have dreamed possible or accessible.

When Sheryl and I began to settle in the church God led us to here in Braintree, there were many things we needed to adjust to. It would become the place from where He purposed us to engage with His plans that would unfold before us. Plans that opened a whole potential of possibilities that would take us to new levels of engagement. But to begin with, the challenge of transition for us involved striking a balance between holding back the 'leader' in us with our own experiences and ideas and still having things to offer from our past ministry that could contribute to and enhance the mission here.

When God determines a purpose for our life and calls us to follow in its path, it is not a haphazard journey that we may or may not stumble upon. He has already gone on ahead of us, preparing and releasing circumstances that ensure we are placed in the way of discerning the vision He has for us; we are then, in cooperation with His Spirit, equipped to release His will in its practical outworking.

However, following Him in this is never based on knowing everything that is ahead and simply being released into it and called to get on with it. When those first disciples began the journey they were invited on, they soon found it was one of continued learning, experiencing, getting things wrong and getting pulled up for it, witnessing and contributing to astonishing things and seeing incredible breakthroughs. It was a journey of ongoing discovery, where their landscape and world view would continuously change in unfamiliar ways as they progressed, and where their eyes needed to be firmly fixed on Jesus. I suggest it is the same for all of us who choose to follow Him. It requires us to travel with Him in proximity, because He seldom gives us the entire picture in advance.

It was the week of Sheryl's birthday. We had made a few plans, which included going out for a meal midweek, followed by an invitation to support someone from our fellowship who was speaking at one of the churches in the neighbouring town. Also, that coming weekend, we had agreed to watch our son playing in a charity football match for the local hospital where he worked. There was in addition a prophetic conference taking place at our church that same weekend, part of which we would miss, watching the football match.

Those were our plans. They were not God's plans. From experience, His plans normally override ours. It just so happened that on the day of our meal, I started to feel quite unwell. By the time we sat down to eat, I was wrestling with the dilemma of not wanting to spoil Sheryl's celebrations but feeling increasingly rough. I muddled through the meal, but my nauseous stomach won out in the end. Say no more. For the remainder of the week, I was largely out of things. Spending Saturday with our son had to be cancelled. I simply did not have the strength to stand through an entire football match.

Then, everything changed. By the time Saturday afternoon arrived, I was feeling considerably better. So much so, I suggested to Sheryl we should go to the prophetic conference that evening. If I started to feel unwell, we were only two minutes' walk from home, so it would not be a problem to withdraw. We went and I was fine all the way through.

The meeting was, as expected, inspirational and uplifting. But that was not the main significance of the event. It was to be a platform for what God was about to launch in ECB. Towards the end of the evening, I sensed the Lord speaking to me with something He wanted me to share with our pastor, then and there.

I'm always conscious of His nudging in these circumstances when I believe He wants something conveyed, because my heart starts to race, my hand starts to shake and I become increasingly fidgety and restless. It is as if there is a divine hand prodding and stabbing me in the back to get up and move. I have learned not to disregard it.

As the evening ended, I shared with my pastor what I was sensing. He, convicted it was a word from God, then invited me to share this with the whole congregation the following day during the morning service, which I did. What I conveyed was exactly as I sensed the Holy Spirit relayed it to me:

> Because you have given me space in this church and allowed my Spirit freedom, I am going to set this church on fire. From here I will then set Manor Street [*where our church is situated*] on fire from one end to the other [*what I saw looked like big flames that started one end and then spread all the way down the centre of the road until they reached the town square*]. And I will then ignite this whole town. I am going to take this town and it begins here in this church. [*I then saw a red open-top sightseeing bus full of people but coming from the town centre down the wrong way of this one-way street. It stopped outside the church and all the people were filing off and going inside. The empty bus then drove off, went round the town and came back again full off people who again got off and went inside the church. This kept repeating again and again.*] This is where it starts. Here in this church.

It was a message that was received with great excitement and anticipation. But, like any prophetic word, there needed to be discernment and a testing of its validity. Was it in line with Scripture or did it contradict what the Word of God said? Did it glorify Jesus and edify His body here, and continue to do so, or was it controlling and manipulative in its nature? And did it sit comfortably with our spirits as a fellowship, in agreement with the accountability of leadership, and reflect the direction the Holy Spirit was leading us in?

These are areas we prayerfully grappled with and explored over a period, frequently returning to it, initially within the leadership team I was invited to share this with and then the wider church. What was increasingly becoming clear was that it carried a purpose and a vision that would begin to unfold in the weeks and months that followed, but would also continue to grow and develop beyond that, as we moved forward in the direction God was leading us.

But it might be worth pausing to consider the nature of God communicating such things to us. You may ask why He does that, or you may have doubts as to whether God still speaks to us directly today in such ways. Why wouldn't He?

We have already seen that any relationship, particularly one as intimate as the relationship God enables us to have with Him, by its very nature requires a two-way dialogue. We do not merely hand God a list of requests when we pray. I would suggest that the true nature of intimacy with Him must surely rest not so much in us pouring out our needs and wants to Him, but in seeking His heart and His will for us. There is always mystery with God. We should not presume to understand His thoughts or His ways other than that which He chooses to disclose to us:

> But as it is written:
> 'Eye has not seen, nor ear heard,
> Nor have entered into the heart of man
> The things which God has prepared for those who love Him.'
> *1 Corinthians 2:9*

We live with the tension of revelation and mystery in our walk with Jesus. Within that tension lies reverence for, fear of and intimacy with the God who is far above all things, yet as near as a breath's whisper:

> Now we have received, not the spirit of the world, but the Spirit who is from God, that we might know the things that have been freely given to us by God.
> *1 Corinthians 2:12*

Having prophetic words from God is one thing. Seeing them come into fruition is quite another. Words of encouragement from God are always welcome, but left there they can fade and disappear, ending as dreams rather than vision.

It is therefore important that we not only hang on to His word when He speaks, but then also engage with Him prayerfully to work through the implications these words hold, until they come into tangible recognition in their fulfilment. Rachel Hickson comments: 'When we have no clarity, we need to stay encamped in our present place; even if it takes a longer time, we must be patient.'[50]

It is not, I believe, His intention that we should passively stand by and wait until something 'happens'. He has given us minds and intellect to engage with Him in the whole process until its realisation is complete; to act upon His word and His direction, and not on impulsive suppositions.

My experience, and Sheryl's, is that God often precedes what He is about to release with revelation that speaks of His intentions to keep us alert to His purposes. We then become watchful in looking for His imprint on unfolding events that He has already announced will happen. In this case, we did not have to wait long.

Sheryl and I had been living in our new house for a few months when we had questions concerning the area, practical

---

[50] Rachel Hickson, *Spiritual Architects* (Oxford: Heartcry for Change, 2020), p104.

things that we wanted to ask the council. It was not a list of complaints, merely things we were unsure of, over which we wanted some clarification. So we wrote to the council, hoping for some answers. What has this to do with the prophetic words I shared in church? We were about to find out.

A representative of the council contacted us and requested to pay us a visit to chat through our enquiries, which we welcomed. How often does that happen? During the ensuing conversation, we stated that we were keen to be involved in participating in community improvements and were not merely running off a list of 'you must do x, y and z'. It was positive, and we were promised a response after he had talked with the various council departments involved.

It never ceases to amaze me how God uses circumstances to unfold His purposes, and draws us into their outworking. While our representative was in his office going through our enquiries, a councillor happened to walk in and asked what he was doing. He explained, and the councillor said he would follow it up and get in touch with us, which he did. One thing led to another, and within a few days Sheryl and I were invited to a meeting with this councillor, our pastor and the chair of the council's voluntary sector for our part of the borough.

The outcome was the setting up of a voluntary group we called Manor Community (Sheryl's suggestion), whose focus would be to enhance Manor Street and the surrounding area for the benefit of both residents and businesses. We felt that as this was worked out, both individual homes and business premises would improve. We know from experience, while engaging with the parish in Rainham, that as practical improvements are made, the atmosphere is changed and community is transformed.

Our desire was to encourage ownership by this community and for residents and neighbours to interact and get to know each other better. We wanted to foster partnership and networking and for this street to be a role model for the whole town. It resonated with the church and the council, and we sensed it was also on God's heart. It was shared with our church leadership team, who were fully behind the scheme, seeing it as an opportunity to embrace the vision as an extension of the church's outreach arm, engaging with and building relationships in the wider community. We invited church members to become involved in the initiatives that would be released, and also encouraged the wider community around us to come on board, and some have.

We began engaging with the street: church volunteers, and one or two others, picking up litter, cleaning verges and offering to tidy up front gardens. We began to build relationships with some of the residents and businesses. We started to notice others in the street tidy up their fronts, put fresh paint on tired walls and woodwork. Then others wider afield started to take notice and we were getting invites to share with wider community groups and community leaders. We held a couple of Saturday coffee mornings in church, to which other councillors came and the conversations and vision spread. Police and fire departments were also taking an interest. We set out a whole schedule of events through the following year for the community to engage with and participate in.

This was a fire, a passion that was beginning to spread, as God's words echoed in our hearts: 'I am going to set this church of fire, then this street on fire and then...' And then... the COVID-19 pandemic hit, lockdown came and everything shut down.

Now, I am aware that through history this nation and this world have undergone many catastrophes, wars, pandemics and disasters. Each one has presented its own set of threats, issues and challenges, where lives were lost, communities disrupted, hardship and health issues escalated and eventually, somehow, the storms were weathered. The human spirit has the capacity to adapt and rise to such challenges. It is more than just survival. There is an intrinsic aspect of our humanity that embraces the nature of hope. It is an inbuilt driving force that will not be denied. So often we see people reach out to God in times of darkness, searching for reassurance when circumstances look dire, like a lost child crying out for their mother or father to come running and grab hold of their hand in reassurance. When we are no longer in control of our circumstances, it is then that we weigh up what is important and what is not. It is here that God can whisper in our spirit that reassurance of His presence, empowering us to press in and push on regardless. This is the nature of our faith in God and why He calls us to draw near to Him, not just in times of difficulty, but as an ongoing relationship that gives us a firm foundation on which to stand firm in whatever storms may come.

> Therefore, having been justified by faith, we have peace with God through our Lord Jesus Christ, though whom also we have access by faith into this grace in which we stand, and rejoice in hope of the glory of God. And not only *that*, but we also glory in tribulations, knowing that tribulation produces perseverance; and perseverance, character; and character, hope. Now hope does not disappoint, because the love of God has been poured out in our hearts by the Holy Spirit who was given to us.
> *Romans 5:1-5*

Hope is bound up in relationships. The need not only for God, but also for one another. The need to be in and part of a community that embraces us and enables us to reach out and touch others. What for me was singled out in the pandemic crisis was the specific way the virus was transmitted from person to person which, as a result, attacked not only our health but our relationships too. We were being kept apart from physical human contact for all the right reasons, but such isolation is unnatural to us. Nothing reinforces the significance of our identity as relational beings more than when we are deprived of it. In an environment where social distancing keeps us from the normality of gathering and interacting, there is a heightened awareness of our need for one another in a social context.

What made this more acute was that isolation heightened our fears and frustrations. Issues of mental health escalated.

Domestic violence saw a huge rise in the cries for help.[51] Vulnerable people were at a greater disadvantage and threat. Those on the front line were at higher risk of falling prey to infection. Frozen economies meant closure for many businesses and unemployment increased as a result. Our human resolve, however, is to rise above these limitations and not be deprived of that which is most important to us – our need for each other. It has not deterred us from engagement.

There is so much we are not in control of, but it has not prevented us from discovering positive outcomes in the restrictions of our circumstances. It has pressed us to look more creatively at how we engage with one another, not just through this crisis, but in the longer term, as society emerges from this season into a new landscape.

It has also created an ongoing platform for dialogue. People are asking questions about their life, the existence of God, what is and is not important in life, issues regarding the stability or instability of our fragile world, and much more. Questions that were never in the forefront of our thoughts in such a way before.

Surviving or thriving?

Life is full of unpredictable surprises, dilemmas and catastrophes, both natural and human made. We have always lived with these uncertainties. Turmoil can come in all manner of ways and from all directions. Events in our lives can change dramatically, and the environment we find ourselves in then throws us off kilter. It might be natural disasters, global health issues or wars. Whatever the cause, the unexpected is to be

---

[51] 'Facts and figures: Ending violence against women', UN Women, www.unwomen.org/en/what-we-do/ending-violence-against-women/facts-and-figures (accessed 24th August 2023); '"The shadow pandemic": gender based violence and Covid –19' Concern Worldwide, www.concern.org.uk/news/shadow-pandemic-gender-based-violence-and-covid-19 (accessed 24th August 2023).

expected. The question is how we respond, especially when we do not appear to have the power or influence to change our circumstances, whether they affect us as individuals, as a community or even on a global scale.

Following Babylon's invasion and conquest of Judah between approximately 605BC and 598BC, many captives, particularly the skilled and educated, found themselves exiled and forced to live under a new regime and culture, totally alien and terrifying. Daniel and his three friends, Hananiah, Mishael and Azariah, would have been teenagers when they were part of the deported entourage. They found themselves in unprecedented times, in a new and different environment and unfamiliar cultural landscape. It could possibly have been to these young and impressionable minds quite seductive, as they looked around the city they were brought to, with its vast, opulent, ornate buildings, palaces, temples and other architectural structures.

The courts where Daniel would serve as a trainee would have been like nothing he had experienced before. Many of his peers may well have succumbed to this visual enticement and been swallowed up wholesale in its identity. But Daniel and his friends remained steadfast and true to their trust in God, despite the tempting and pressurised influences to draw them away from their faith to be shaped by a new cultural and religious world view that sought to impose its own ideology upon them.[52]

Adjusting and adapting to new circumstances is challenging for any of us at the best of times. More so when such an environment we find ourselves in is hostile, unpredictable and alien to our perceived way of life. It takes courage, resolve and confidence in ourselves to overcome the obstacles we then face and need to engage with. That may not be so arduous if we know the situation is short and transitory. But when there is no end in sight and no guarantee of how we may come out the other side, or what the future will look like, our mental and

---

[52] Daniel 1:2, 4, 8.

spiritual attitude and strength will determine whether we enter such a season with a positive or negative outlook.

Daniel would have had no idea at that stage that his entire life would now be lived out in this new environment. The most important thing he would hold on to, if he were to protect and maintain his identity, was his faith in God, drawing close in trust and in the knowledge that he would not be abandoned.

The issue is whether we survive or thrive in such circumstances. The nature of following Jesus may well challenge how we envisage God building and directing His Church in such an uncertain environment as we find ourselves in today. Our outlook and attitude may be relevant here, but there is another aspect that is perhaps more important than living through the ordeal as best we can. It is the fact that God has a purpose for our lives, directed by Him and not by our circumstances, even though we may be affected by them. It is a purpose often bigger than and different from what we may expect or perceive.

When Jesus calls us to follow Him into an unknown future that He holds for us, we bring into that journey ourselves, our past experiences of life, our gifts and abilities, our characters and personalities, our hopes and dreams, our anxieties and fears and little else. Remember, those first disciples of Jesus left everything to follow Him. It is who we are that is then shaped to become who we are created to be and the destiny we are born for. This is then the ongoing reality released by His relational guidance through the interaction of His Holy Spirit living in us. To engage in such a faith-filled journey will be beset by issues of hostility, misunderstanding and opposition because, by its very nature, to follow Jesus in the true sense of discipleship requires us to forego our identity in a worldly context.

Jesus leads us on a path that bears fruit, but it also carries with it difficulties, challenges and opposition. His agenda and His purpose for us are what underline the route we take. Its direction and outcome may not be clear when we set out, but it is not totally unknown, because as we step along its path in obedient faith and trust, a path known to Him and ordained by

Him, so His intentions come into reality with ever-increasing clarity.

Discipleship does not necessarily make us immune from pressures to conform to worldly views and values, however contrary they are to the kingdom identity we are called to walk in and embrace. We can easily be drawn into compromise or dilute who we are in Christ in favour of a more comfortable walk that demands little of us.

We can buy into a culture that slowly and subtly diminishes our integrity as followers, removing the impact, influence and power we have, while reducing our following to a consumer-based religion devoid of any relevance that can change the world around us.

This was certainly the world Daniel and his friends found themselves in, and there is much their steadfastness can teach us in terms of being rooted and standing firm in the faith we have, while at the same time allowing God to fully use us in the places and environment where we have been positioned.

Stepping into the unfamiliar

I suspect there are many who found the COVID-19 crisis to be one of feeling robbed or bereft of things that were not only familiar to our way of life, but also fundamental to our structures of living. Until restrictions were eased, we were unable to gather in our church buildings, separated from one another physically. We were left to rethink how we might pastorally care for one another or worship together or continue past missional initiatives that had been put on hold. It is in such circumstances, in what appears as darkness, that faith comes to the fore, where we discover the rock on which we stand.

Daniel and his friends were brought into this new environment for the purpose that God had ordained for them. It was not what they would have expected nor necessarily chosen, but they would be used mightily and influentially by Him. Like Daniel, we are not called by God merely to survive, but to thrive. In an environment that disempowers, God is here empowering, assuring, encouraging and filling us. He has not, and does not, abandon us regardless of our circumstances, however dire things may appear to be. Whether navigating through a pandemic and beyond, or any other unfamiliar and hostile environment we may find ourselves in, the God of the universe, who has no equal, walks alongside us. He has purpose for us. He is fully in control.

There may be challenging times ahead for the Church, but I believe this can be a season of empowerment. Creating an environment of anticipation and expectation is important, because I believe the wind of His Spirit is blowing over us again, so that we may see amazing breakthrough. Expect God to act. New circumstances, new opportunities, new landscapes and a new harvest ready to be gathered in; I believe it is a season of encouragement for the people of God, amid all the uncertainties that lie ahead. I believe, also, there is no going back.

> Do not remember the former things,
> Nor consider the things of old.
> Behold, I will do a new thing,
> Now it shall spring forth;
> Shall you not know it?
> I will even make a road in the wilderness
> *And* rivers in the desert ...
> To give drink to My people, My chosen.
> *Isaiah 43:18-20*

Thought break

- Where do you find hope to be most evident? What is your confidence in life based on?

- Do you see yourself at this moment in your life as surviving or thriving? What draws you to that conclusion?

- How do you cope with unexpected changes? Are you motivated by challenges that take you to new places or threatened by them? Why?

8

Maintaining Identity

The nature of our discipleship is designed to define our identity in Christ, transforming us to be like Him and enabling us to engage with His purposes for our lives. Thereby we increasingly display His nature and release His will to have an impact on the world around us.

I wonder what would have become of Daniel and his friends had Babylon not invaded Judah and they had not been deported to the new environment they found themselves in. It's an interesting thought, but not necessarily superfluous. Sometimes things must shift for us to be released into the potential to which we are called. The integrity of our unique identity, not our circumstances, is what remains fundamental to fulfilling the intentions God has for us.

Following Him means He chooses the setting into which He brings our distinctive calling. Sheryl and I could have moved anywhere in our retirement. The only limitation we placed geographically was to be within a reasonable distance of our children and grandchildren. That is still a lot of places we could have moved to. But we were led to a town that wasn't on our radar and of which we knew very little. Yet this was where He chose us to be. Our destiny in God's hands is always strategic, in both timing and location. You and I are here for a purpose and a time such as no other; uniquely ours. Our placement lies within the nature of our following.

Transformation is not about becoming another person for another situation, but being enriched in who we already are, enhanced to be fruitful in the context in which we are placed or find ourselves. When we choose to follow Jesus, we are equipped and sent to release the kingdom of God into our world, wherever we are located, to proclaim the good news, to make disciples and to change the cultural environment around us, that it may increasingly reflect the love and glory of God. We are in that sense an apostolic Church. We are a sent people.

Our assignment has not changed since Jesus called and transformed those first disciples, even though our circumstances may have. We are called to change the atmosphere around us, from fear and anxiety to hope and promise… the environment of heaven; the advancement of the kingdom of God, beckoning us to 'repent' (change direction) and 'believe' (Mark 1:15).

I want to remind you that you are significant. You are valued and precious. You are called for a purpose. But like Daniel and his friends, our circumstances living in a world that increasingly has turned its back on God can easily erode who we are in Christ. Our identity, our lifestyle choices and our effectiveness as the body of Christ can shape the impact we have and the influence we generate. Our deep-rootedness is central to ensuring this journey we take with Jesus keeps our eyes firmly fixed on Him and not on the world that tries to prise us away from Him.

Names reflect identity

Have you ever thought about your name? It is more than simply what your parents decided to call you when you were born. In our modern Western society, that may not appear so relevant, because sometimes parents choose their child's name based on popularity or current trends without necessarily thinking about its significance. But in many cultures in history and even today, names are chosen to reflect the nature or character that underlines them. They speak about identity or association with significant origins, giving them a greater place of belonging and ownership of the personality they convey. We see it with several biblical people whose names God changed to reflect their new calling, status and character. Abram became Abraham, the 'father of many nations' (Genesis 17:5); Jacob became Israel because he 'struggled with God and with men, and ... prevailed' (Genesis 32:28); Simon became Peter, whose declaration reflected the 'rock' on which the faith of the Church is built (Matthew 16:18). That is not always the case, though. Some names in the Bible already have significant meaning reflecting a correlation with God. Daniel, Hananiah, Mishael and Azariah were theophoric names linked to their identity in this way, that contained attributes to the names of God. But it was Ashpenaz, master of the eunuchs, whose charge they were under, who changed their names to Belteshazzar, Shadrach, Meshach and Abed-Nego.[53] Perhaps this was an attempt to further eradicate association with or identity in any reference to the one true God of Israel, and instead bear mention to Babylonian gods, thus further indoctrinating them into the ways of the Chaldeans.

Who we are is significant, as is our name. But knowing whose we are and not just who we are underpins strength of character, giving our identity meaning and purpose. Did you know your identity and purpose, mapped out for your whole life, was written in God's book of life long before you were created? He knew you and saw you before you were born:

> Your eyes saw my substance, being yet unformed.
> And in Your book they all were written,
> The days fashioned for me,
> When *as yet there were* none of them.
> *Psalm 139:16*

Moreover, when you respond to the call of Jesus to follow Him, your life takes on a whole new meaning; that which was

---

[53] Daniel 1:6-7.

ordained for you, 'written in [His] Book' (Revelation 21:27). That is His will for you and me, but to implement it, we must step into that calling, surrendering our will to His, and embrace the relationship we are summoned to walk in.

We did not choose Him, but He us.[54] We are called by His name. 'Everyone who is called by My name, Whom I have created for My glory; I have formed him, yes, I have made him' (Isaiah 43:7). It is this, I believe, that bears reference to the relationship between the shepherd and his sheep that Jesus speaks of:

> To him the doorkeeper opens, and the sheep hear his voice; and he calls his own sheep by name and leads them out. And when he brings out his own sheep, he goes before them; and the sheep follow him, for they know his voice.
> *John 10:3-4*

That is our place of belonging and our identity. Our lives are written in His book. He knows each of us personally by name, and calls us by name. Not only that, but in such a relationship, we also know Him and identify with Him. We recognise His voice above all the other voices clamouring for our attention in the chaotic busyness of our world.

Focus on who God says you are and not on who others or the world say you are. You are a child of God, a son or daughter of a loving heavenly Father, adopted into His family. You are a child of the King who reigns over all things. He bought you for a heavy price, paid by His Son, Jesus. This is your identity. This is who you are.

Dumping the junk food

Daniel became unsettled in his spirit. Something was niggling him and making him feel uncomfortable. Why? After all, he was

---

[54] John 15:16.

daily being offered all kinds of delicacies to eat and wines to drink; a wide palette of sumptuous foods fit for the king. He would have lacked for nothing. And yet it all felt wrong.

> But Daniel purposed in his heart that he would not defile himself with the portion of the king's delicacies, nor with the wine which he drank; therefore he requested of the chief of the eunuchs that he might not defile himself.
> *Daniel 1:8*

He did not want to taint himself with this luxury, because the king's food and drink would have been dedicated to idols and Daniel felt that this would have compromised his relationship with God. It is why he petitioned the chief of the eunuchs for an alternative diet, assuring him that it would not hinder his health or affect his duties in the court.

So what, you might think. Is it such a big deal, what we eat and what we don't eat? After all, in a global economy, do we really know where our food is processed, where it comes from, what it contains? We are all aware of healthy and unhealthy diets when it comes to eating and drinking. If it is just nourishment we are talking about, then perhaps it may not be significant, other than affecting our physical health. But we are more than what we eat.

There is a spiritual dimension at play here. For Daniel, this was perhaps another attempt to distance him from his God and undermine his integrity in the faith he held so strongly; a faith he was not willing to sacrifice. Paul also alludes to this concept in 1 Corinthians 8:7-9, regarding food offered to idols as potentially bringing defilement, especially to those who are weak in their faith and easily swayed to wander into areas that are unhealthy. Daniel was not weak in his faith but was not willing to even consider such a compromise.

It is perhaps not so much the food that is the issue, but our attitude towards our lifestyle before the God who calls us to follow Him. How we live affects how we respond to life's issues and challenges and how empowered we are to deal with the things we are confronted with. It becomes a matter of inner strength and having our spiritual roots firmly planted in our relationship with Jesus.

What do you feed on? What sustains you and gives you that inner strength? There are all kinds of diets we 'feed on' that can affect our way of life, our emotional and spiritual health as well as our physical well-being. They are all interrelated and have an impact on who we are and how we live.

We can, and often do, buy into all kinds of unhealthy things that are appealing and enticing but not necessarily beneficial. The media, for example, is quite good at feeding us a worldly diet of pessimism and scepticism, creating fear, anxiety and doubt about what may be already difficult situations for some, and this with little regard to how those in their vulnerability may respond or be affected.

Likewise, maintaining a culture of popularity and acceptability, in pursuit of material gain to 'keep up with the Joneses', can leave us unfulfilled and on a constant cycle of wanting or needing more, because we quickly become dissatisfied with what we have. Such is the nature of our human self-consciousness. We do not want to miss out on what is on offer: a world full of promise that so often fails to provide or satisfy.

Maintaining a healthy spiritual lifestyle and rhythm are paramount in our walk of discipleship if we are to stay on course on the path set before us by the One we seek to follow: 'And Jesus said to them, "I am the bread of life. He who comes to Me shall never hunger, and he who believes in Me shall never thirst"' (John 6:35). Jesus alone is the One who meets all our needs and satisfies all our desires. So how do we feed on Him?

We can develop a practice of spiritual feeding by regularly spending time with His Word and allowing His Spirit to bring it to life. Wisdom, knowledge and understanding of our relationship with God release strength and confidence, not just in knowing who He is, but also in who we are, and are therefore as important to our health and well-being as eating physical food, if not more so. I am not talking here about just dipping into a Bible as a tick-box exercise, but of fully immersing ourselves in His Word. I have often said that Scripture is not a book, but a dialogue with God. Asking Him to speak to us and to provide insight is the starting point to opening the pages we engage with, not in head knowledge so much as heart knowledge. It is the personhood of Jesus we feed on, not a set of rules or guidelines to life. It is here, surely, that we flourish and prosper, deep-rooted and steeped in His Word.

This is the nature of the disciple's intimacy with Jesus: to be immersed in His presence night and day, feeding on His Word, walking in dialogue with Him, conscious of His indwelling presence in us in every circumstance where we find ourselves and every conversation that we have with whoever we engage with.

God is continually positioning us for His purpose to release His living reality in and through us in empowerment and authority, so we may further His kingdom in the process of our everyday lives and make Him more visible to others. I wonder what people would say if you were to ask them, 'Who do you see when you're looking at me?' Who do you think they see?

A time of favour

'And whatever he does shall prosper' (Psalm 1:3). God's purpose for us carries with it favour so we may prosper in fruitfulness. Sometimes we must make a stand when we are challenged with compromises that undermine our faith. It is in standing firm amid temptations to pull us away from God that we discover the release of something greater that enhances our walk with Him and places us in influential positions.

When Daniel made a stand against what was being forced on him, God honoured that commitment. 'Now God had brought Daniel into the favor and goodwill of the chief of the eunuchs' (Daniel 1:9). How did that pan out? The eunuch agreed to Daniel's suggestion of a trial period of dieting on vegetables followed by a review after ten days. At the end of that trial period, Daniel and his friends appeared fuller and healthier than those who maintained the king's diet. God then increased their knowledge, skills, understanding and wisdom so that they became more prominent than all the king's magicians and astrologers in his realm; not just a little bit, but 'ten times better' than the others in all matters (Daniel 1:19,20). That, I would suggest, carries a lot of influential weight in the courts of power.

Putting on spiritual weight is the product of our intimacy with Jesus and the result of our investing time with Him. Notice when Jesus calls disciples, He does so in the context of community, not a group of individuals in collective. We are called to be in relationship with one another as well as with Him.

Our spiritual well-being is incumbent upon each one of us encouraging one another with a healthy diet, sharing words He lays on our heart with others and feeding one another, even asking God to give us encouraging words for those who might be struggling. It is a time to grow in maturity and depth, because I believe this is a season and environment where we carry favour and can be influential in our towns and neighbourhoods, perhaps like never before.

In this season, there is an openness in our community to build relationships and bridges and to engage with what I call people of peace.[55] The fluidity of the world we now occupy has made that possible because its instability and fragility has been laid bare by the circumstances that we find ourselves in. What was is no longer and what will be has not yet surfaced. It has the potential to make everyone receptive to new possibilities and new truths they had not explored or considered before.

Sheryl and I, as well as others, have found that in engaging with our neighbours and others in our community, there is much more of an openness to conversations about faith, where gestures of kindness and support have created an atmosphere that enables relationships to grow closer. Such investment in people carries with it fruitfulness.

---

[55] Luke 10:5-9.

In the time we have been living in Braintree, we have seen the benefits of those relationships we have built with our neighbours; not just those living either side of us, but also increasingly further along our street. People are starting to look beyond the confines of a materialistic world. Some have even asked us to pray for them, bringing their concerns, anxieties and fears to the fore in the confidence and trust that we have something to offer that is genuine and tangible. In addition, we are in a season of seeing a strengthening of our relationships with the local authority, and especially those with whom we are working closely. This has resulted in a positive and practical response to some local needs and issues.

There is an increasing hunger for something, or 'someone', that can bring hope, peace and direction with a foundation that is strong and immovable. I believe that as disciples of Jesus, we carry influence and favour in the community and especially among community leaders, guiding and pointing them to that source – Jesus Christ. I believe key figures in the community will come to us as the body of Christ for wise counsel and advice, making the Church instrumental and influential in the way forward.

God is positioning His Church for purpose. And as in Daniel's circumstances, He is bringing us onto a new pathway and into a new setting, to gather in a new harvest.

> Do you not say, 'There are still four months and *then* comes the harvest'? Behold, I say to you, lift up your eyes and look at the fields, for they are already white for harvest!'
> *John 4:35*

Thought break

- What most of all gives you the confidence that your identity is in Jesus and that is where you belong?

- If you are not yet in that place of knowing, what do you believe would draw you closer to discovering that truth?

- What are the things that you feed on in your everyday life? How 'nourishing' or fulfilling do you find them? How healthy is your spiritual diet?

- Are there areas in your life that compromise your faith? How might you strengthen your commitment to Jesus? What might Daniel's example teach you?

9

Faith Walks on Water

Consider for a moment the word 'faith'. What does it speak of to you? I would suggest that, primarily, it involves confidently putting our trust in a person or persons, or a concept or situation, we believe to be true or reliable. As a result, we assure ourselves that we are doing the right thing, even if we don't see visible evidence to back up our decision. But that can come across in quite a vague or naïve way. Does it, for example, explain the necessity of believing, or the degree to which belief or trust in that something or someone needs to be exercised? Does it give any underpinning guarantees as to the outcome of exercising genuine faith to step into what we believe to be true and appropriate? Possibly not.

We all believe in something, however obscure or abstract a concept that may appear to be. Some of our beliefs are rational; others less so. I would suggest much of our lives are built on some form of faith, whether it be in ourselves and our abilities, our dreams and our aspirations, or on external circumstances that are outside our control and may or may not come to pass, even though we pin our hopes on them.

Many of the choices we make and decisions we take require an element of faith or trust, to believe that we have made the right decision based on the evidence or information we have. Even everyday simple tasks require us to step out in faith. If, for example, I am crossing the road from the place of assuring myself that there are no cars coming, I can trust that I will be safe in crossing without putting myself in danger. If I perform the same task without looking or listening for traffic, that will be reckless and hazardous. But what happens when we are required to step out of familiar settings and out of our comfort zones; where faith is the only thing we are hanging on by; where the only way we can respond is to move in its path, without knowing the outcome? What about when we put that faith in a person who beckons us to follow Him without the slightest notion of the implications that may involve? Because this is the kind of faith Jesus requires of us if we are to commit ourselves to His purpose for our lives. Faith, in this context, only becomes real when we step into its unknown territory without a guarantee and without necessarily seeing what lies ahead. When Jesus calls us to follow Him, this is the journey of faith we undertake.

There comes a point when we need to understand that our relationship with Jesus is not like that of a coach who shouts instructions to an athlete from the sideline to push harder, but rather a co-athlete running alongside, or a co-fisherman, or a teaching colleague, or whatever it is we are engaged with. He is there, always alongside and within us, to show us more and release us more into the realms of the impossible.

There are times when we get that and, as a result, fly in remarkable ways, seeing ministries propelled forward with unprecedented fruitfulness. But often as not, we return to our 'norm' and the old mindset kicks in. Perhaps those disciples who witnessed Jesus alive again following His resurrection fell into that way of thinking. The fishermen went back to their old occupation and again set out to fish. Having spent the night on the lake and catching nothing, you would have thought the penny would have dropped. They had been there before. But it took a voice from the shoreline that morning to wake them up to their new reality. Perhaps they were not really paying attention when, at the start of His ministry, He invited them to follow Him and in so doing they would 'catch men' (Luke 5:10). So, here at the other end of that ministry, it needed a gentle and subtle reminder:

> But when the morning had now come, Jesus stood on the shore; yet the disciples did not know that it was Jesus. Then Jesus said to them, 'Children, have you any food?' They answered Him, 'No.'
> And He said to them, 'Cast the net on the right side of the boat, and you will find *some*.' So they cast, and now they were not able to draw it in because of the multitude of fish.
> *John 21:4-6*

Having shared breakfast on the beach with them, Jesus then pulled Simon Peter to one side to redress the howler this impetuous disciple had made in denying he knew Jesus in the courtyard of the high priest, during Jesus' arrest and trial. 'Do you love Me …?' (John 21:15-17). It's not easy being asked that just once, but three times! The point had to be made. After all, Peter had vehemently denied having anything to do with Jesus more than once. But I feel this was more than a restoration, as significant as that was. It was also a reminder of what Peter, and the others, were called to – to care for, pastor and teach others, discipling them onto the pathway of following. Peter did not need rebuking but restoring. He did not receive correction but love.

The question of whether Peter loved Jesus was a foil to how much Jesus loved him (and each one of us), and the price He paid in demonstrating it. Love costs, and all that Peter was called to and reinstated in would cost him too, as Jesus informed him in John 21:18-19.

How many times have we done that? Denied knowing Jesus or been unwilling to step into the frame that makes our declaration transparent? Consciously or subconsciously, we can often exclude Jesus from our lives and carry on as if He does not matter, or we lose sight of His presence, preventing others from seeing Him in us. We again become preoccupied with the demands and pursuits of our earthly normality.

There are so many ways we can live our lives in a secular environment and framework, where Jesus is relegated to an afterthought, a 'private' relationship, or one that is only visible in the context of our church gatherings. There can be no going back to old and familiar patterns of life when we commit to follow Him.

Boat rides on a lake

Being transformed as a disciple is a process that takes us from our known and familiar environment to experiences and encounters that embrace a whole different set of criteria. It is the realm of the supernatural. You think you know someone until something completely throws that understanding of them out of the window.

Pause for a moment. What does 'supernatural' mean to you? It is perhaps best described as something beyond the realm of our physical/natural experience. For example, if I drop a glass that is in my hand, it will fall to the floor. That is natural. If I let go of it and it remains floating in mid-air, that is supernatural.

The supernatural is God's natural – they are inseparable to Him. To put this into context, Jesus became a man and stepped into our world to enable us to engage with Him on a human level, but not simply on human terms. To do that, He needed to bring His world into ours, to demonstrate what His kingdom looks like and how it operates. His world is as different from ours as light is to darkness. His call to follow Him necessarily means embracing His world and operating from that perspective. 'For with God nothing will be impossible' (Luke 1:37). Easier said than done, but not impossible.

There is another encounter the disciples experienced on water, in Matthew 14:22-33.

It was familiar territory for many of them, who would have crossed over the lake countless times. But this was no ordinary or familiar episode. It was another learning curve; another fusion of ordinary and extraordinary; another stretching of faith, expanding their perception of Jesus and themselves even further.

The encounter took place immediately after Jesus miraculously fed a multitude of 5,000-plus people with two fish and five barley loaves. This was on the back of Jesus initially instructing His disciples to feed the crowd when they wanted to send them away into the neighbouring villages to get food. 'But Jesus said to them, "They do not need to go away. You give them something to eat"' (Matthew 14:16).

It is an obvious and common response to look at meeting such a need with an earthly perspective and solution. That is all they could offer; that which could be found physically. And the divine exchange then multiplied what they offered. It is the point where the impossible meets the possible and the two are intertwined in the miraculous. It is the principle upon which our discipleship is founded, placing what we have into the hands of Jesus and experiencing what He can do with it, in cooperation and partnership.

But, returning to the lake, did they grasp what was going on? Did they fully comprehend what He was showing and teaching them, the dynamics involved when it comes to releasing the resources of heaven to fulfil an earthly need?

Jesus sends them off in a boat to the other side of the lake while He remains behind. He goes off by Himself to spend time with His Father. By the time He finishes praying, it is night. The boat with the disciples is still making its way to the other side and is now in the middle of the lake, when an ensuing storm is starting to toss them about.

In the early hours of the morning, Jesus approaches them, walking on the water. It is dark. The wind is howling around them. The waves are leaping up and the boat is being tossed around like it is on a roller coaster. The sea is probably spraying in their faces and visibility is poor.

In all that, they catch a glimpse of a shape, a figure of some sort, coming towards them. They do not make any connection and fail to recognise the figure as Jesus. Why would they?

Walking on the water is the last place they would have expected to see Him. But there He is, moving closer and closer amid all the buffeting they are receiving. The disciples freak out in fear, assuming they are seeing a ghost or an apparition of some sort.

It is interesting how often fear of the unknown brings into our consciousness an alternate rationale when we cannot find a practical or physical explanation of something abnormal that we experience. We can send our minds into overdrive with all kinds of envisaged explanations that leave us trembling with fright or anxiety. It does not even have to be sinister. But when we cannot explain something unexpected, it defies our logic and leaves us bewildered.

How often did Jesus have to tell His disciples not to be afraid? They had so many encounters of unexpected and unnatural events taking place which Jesus instigated, yet it did not make it any easier. So here again, Jesus must reassure them. 'But immediately Jesus spoke to them, saying, "Be of good cheer! It is I; do not be afraid"' (Matthew 14:27). Or to put it another way: 'Hey, guys, chill! It's Me; take it easy; it's cool.'

Jesus did not gather disciples to follow Him merely as spectators or as a fan club. They were there to engage with Him in the realm He operated from – heaven. So here was their next work experience assignment. Perhaps Peter wanted to double check it really was Jesus when he tested what was said, along the lines of, 'OK, if you're genuinely here on the water, then I should be able to come out to you if you call me, right?' Jesus beckoned him out of the boat to come to Him, which Peter obligingly did. His eyes were fixed on Jesus. He was focused and full of trust as he climbed out of the boat and began to make his way towards Jesus, defying the natural and stepping into the supernatural.

This is like my portrayal of the glass floating in mid-air, the glass that should have dropped. This is Peter standing on the surface of a lake, in the middle of a storm. Oh yes, the storm! For a fleeting second Peter took his eyes off Jesus and 'remembered' where he was: on a lake in a storm. It just took a second for his reality to supersede heaven's reality. Like the glass, he dropped, crashing through the tossing waves, and panic again consumed him.

Just for a moment, Peter stepped into the realm of the impossible and it became possible. Yes, the wind was billowing around him, but he already knew that. The storm's reality had succumbed to another reality, just briefly enough for him to experience it first-hand.

So why did he doubt? 'And immediately Jesus stretched out *His* hand and caught him, and said to him, "O you of little faith, why did you doubt?"' (Matthew 14:31). Stepping into His realm requires faith, yes, but how much faith? Is it in amounts or in conviction? After all, Jesus said that we can move mountains, with faith as small 'as a mustard seed' (Matthew 17:20).

I would suggest that releasing faith requires not just conviction, but also confidence and boldness in the One we are following and the word He releases in us. It comes from the place of intimacy, from His heart to ours. Even if only momentarily, Peter's faith was released when Jesus said, 'Come,' long enough for him to action that word in trust.

It was there, and then it wasn't. Peter experienced first-hand what that faith embraces, as he stepped out of his world view and into Jesus', walking, in defiance of science, on water. If Jesus' call to follow requires embracing His world in ours, how do we do that? Where do we place our trust? Because that is the issue.

Paul unashamedly declares that the gospel has power to change lives, and to enter that relationship with God means that we are called to live by faith:

> For I am not ashamed of the gospel of Christ, for it is the power of God to salvation for everyone who believes, for the Jew first and also for the Greek. For in it the righteousness of God is revealed from faith to faith; as it is written, 'The just shall live by faith.'
> *Romans 1:16-17*

Faith has a purpose. It is to draw us closer to God.

The miraculous, the supernatural, the signs and wonders and the like are not there as some sort of sideshow, like that of illusionists or magicians performing unexplainable feats to wow and dazzle a crowd. They are to demonstrate a reality that brings us into a restored relationship with the God of the universe, so we may discover who He is and live in a way that embraces His realm of love, described by Jesus as 'the kingdom of God' (Luke 21:31) or 'the kingdom of heaven' (Matthew 10:7).

It is difficult to live committed to two domains that are contrary to one another. We must embrace the reality of one or the other. There is a clash when we try to embrace both, as Peter discovered on the lake.

If following Jesus requires us to be transformed, to be more and more like Him, then it means entering more and more into His reality until it becomes our default position. The more we experience and operate there, the more natural it becomes. This is the nature of following. Until then, we will always see the storm instead of the call to walk on water. He is on the water and calls us there to step out and take risks. Walking on water means keeping our eyes fixed on Him, not on our surroundings.

This is not just a 'sink or swim' issue, but the need for a change of mindset, a shift in our thinking as to whether we live in total surrender to His will and purpose and allow the relationship He calls us to grow in to govern our perspective and expectation. Do we choose to live under our fear or under His peace? His peace 'surpasses all understanding' (Philippians 4:7) because it is not governed by our circumstances.[56]

Stepping out of the boat can take on many forms in our lives, but each requires the same trust, the same walk of faith, with our eyes fixed on His, and our willingness to take risks. When we step out over the precipice, it is His voice that whispers, 'Don't look down! Look at Me. Keep your eyes fixed on Me.' That needs to be our constant prayer: to be continually

---

[56] John 14:27.

reminded to fix our gaze on Jesus. Only then can we fully submit in obedience to His will. R T Kendall writes: 'God is looking for a people who want to know his ways, his heart and his Word so well that they can learn to pray according to his will.'[57] So often we operate from a consumerist mentality. We want to remain in the safety of the boat, where little is expected of us other than weathering the odd storm.

Sheryl and I love holidays abroad, visiting new places and discovering new historical sites. We loved at one point going to the Italian lakes. Our first time was when we had booked a holiday on the shores of Lake Como. As the holiday was soon to start, we discovered we were going to have our first child and were full of excitement. But we wanted to keep our news to ourselves until we got back.

We so enjoyed our time by the lake, without a care in the world and so much to look forward to. The weather was glorious, the views stunning with the backdrop of the mountains over a sun-kissed lake that sparkled in the afternoon light, like precious jewels glistening on the surface of the shimmering water. We would lie on the lakeside beach, enjoy boat rides across to the other side, and have romantic dinners on the balcony overlooking the lake as the sun went down. It was the perfect unspoilt holiday.

I wonder if perhaps our expectations of following Jesus can be a bit like that: enjoying the view, chilling, soaking up the atmosphere, letting others do the work for us. But comfort-zone boat rides are not what we are called to engage in. We are disciples, not tourists. We were never called to travel in the comfort of a boat, but to walk on the waterways of the impossible paths that He travels on.

This is the basis of faith. It should bring us into the kind of fellowship with Jesus that frees us from restrictive earthly outlooks and, instead, binds us to Him alone and the perspective He enables us to experience. This means stepping

---

[57] R T Kendall, *Out of the Comfort Zone* (London: Hodder & Stoughton, 2005), p33.

into what may appear as insecurity and following in total trust and reliance on Jesus. It is not until such a step of faith is taken into that unknown and perhaps insecure environment that the 'miracles' of His world are released into ours. But to do this, we must consciously be aware of our own weaknesses and limitations, while recognising His almighty power in us.

Faith does not have a safety net, just a voice beckoning, 'Come, step out of the boat, take the risk.' It is a response of obedience to His voice and His call. Dietrich Bonhoeffer, the German theologian, put it like this: 'Faith is only real when there is obedience, never without it and it only becomes so when it is acted upon.' And, 'It means that we can only take this step aright if we fix our eyes not on the work we do, but on the word with which Jesus calls us to do it.'[58]

We always live in the tension of the reality of His world and that of ours clashing in our everyday life experiences. We are always left with the challenge of in what or in whom we place our trust. Is it His Word, or the environment that challenges that Word? There will always be whispers of doubt in our ear, 'Has God indeed said ...?' (Genesis 3:1). The storms around us will always shout for our attention and response. We will always experience fear and anxiety pressing in to intimidate us. But by allowing His Holy Spirit to transform our perception, we will increasingly find ourselves in a position and with an attitude whereby we echo Jesus' own reliance on His relationship with His Father through the Holy Spirit, in doing and saying what we hear and see Him do.[59] It is always on His terms, because with Him 'all things are possible' (Matthew 19:26).

When Sheryl and I took on the leadership of the parish of Rainham and Wennington, it appeared at the start to be a daunting prospect. It was my first incumbency, after several years in teaching, and a short eighteen-month interlude at another church in Collier Row, Romford, where the Bishop of

---

[58] Dietrich Bonhoeffer, *The Cost of Discipleship* (London: SCM Press, 2001), p21,23.
[59] John 5:19; 8:26,28.

Barking placed us to discern the way forward. Our time in Collier Row was invaluable, because of the strength of leadership we were under and the close-knit fellowship that we experienced. It was a wonderful model to equip us and inspire us for what lay ahead. It was, in some respects, our comfortable boat, because we did not at that stage have any pressures of leadership responsibility, even though we engaged in leadership involvement. We were being fed and built up. But it was not the place we were to remain, even though tempting invitations were made. Our prime focus was always to build something 'new'. We were looking for some form of church plant initially, when we spoke to the bishop concerning a future placement. We had a freedom while at Collier Row to engage in practical ways with the things that we were passionate about in ministry. As part of their strategy, we led a church plant in one of the local secondary schools and were able to develop strong team ministry relationships, some that would remain with us beyond our time there.

So when we stepped into Rainham for the first time, it was like stepping out of the boat. Not that we went into it with our eyes closed; far from it. Months before the appointment, we were given prophetic words about leading that church, even before there was a vacancy. And then over several weeks, there were multiple confirmations of God's intention for us to be there.

We were, at one stage, organising a prayer evening, and in preparation I was looking up images of the area on the internet to act as a focal point for our prayers. I typed in 'Collier Row' and only one image appeared. It was a picture of a bus with 'Rainham' written on the front, as its terminus. We were clear that Rainham was the ministry God intended for us for the foreseeable future. But on the day of my licensing, Sheryl and I looked at each other with a questioning gaze that expressed a kind of, 'Are we sure about this?' It was, after all, my first incumbency and in many ways we were stepping into the unknown, even though we knew God's hand was on it. There were some issues that needed to be addressed, as there are in every church, but we were confident we had a good team alongside us to move forward. However, it would not be long before that was to change.

The support mechanism we had inherited in the form of a leadership team started to unravel. Church planters who oversaw one of the outreach communities decided it was time for them to leave the area. We had no replacement and had to put together a makeshift team to continue the work. Our associate minister developed heart problems and was temporarily laid off. Our Lay Reader had debilitating health problems that increasingly prevented them from a lot of the ministry they were engaged in. Sheryl and I found ourselves trying to cover three church communities in two parishes almost single-handedly, while overseeing and implementing strategies to help us cope.

Rainham was itself an area that was deprived in many ways and considered by many as a dumping ground in the borough. There was low self-esteem, even among professional people, and within the community a resigned disposition that was rooted in 'nothing will change here'. It seemed like an uphill, daunting prospect, but we had a clear vision that the Lord had given us, which was summed up with what became our mission statement: 'Putting the community in touch with Jesus'.

This was our focus for the next twelve years. It was fuelled by a compassion that God gave us for the people there and in the neighbouring hamlet of Wennington, the other parish we were responsible for. We grew to love them and were committed to discipling them and releasing them to discover their place in His purposes.

As a priority, we sought to enable the members of the body of Christ in their different settings (the three church communities were quite different from each other) to each have a personal relationship with God as Father through Jesus Christ; to grow in maturity as His disciples and to be equipped by His Spirit to be proactive in God's mission to the wider community.

We also aimed to encourage and develop all-member ministry through a 'team' approach, enabling individuals to discover and grow in their gifting and calling as part of the wider vision; to be kingdom-centred and Spirit-led, ensuring our mission always took precedence over maintenance; we were conscious of utilising all our resources in enabling us in the things we birthed, developed and established. In doing so we wanted to engage with and have an impact on the wider community we were a part of. It was not all plain sailing and not everyone caught the vision. But those who did, we saw grow in maturity and influence, taking on their own ministries in the process.

'Stepping out of the boat', or out of our comfort zone (the familiar and trusted), and taking risks, as we have just seen, requires us to keep our eyes fixed in total trust on Jesus. This is not a blind faith, because we are acting upon His Word and His command and from a place of relationship, not a place of hopeful speculation with fingers crossed. He continually raises the bar of expectation and stretches our faith to increase our strength in reliance and trust upon who He is. Why? Because He wants to release in us the fullness of His kingdom, that He might continue through us to change the world.

We need to be mindful that there are implications for us if we remain in our comfort zones. How different might things be if we choose to 'step out of the boat'? What could the possibilities release, in and through His Church, and where might that take us? There is only one way we can discover that.

Thought break

- Have you ever had to exercise faith in a situation you had no control over but knew you had to step into? What was the outcome? What is the difference between putting faith in yourself ('I can do this') with the belief that things will somehow work out, and putting your faith in Jesus' word?

- Why, by definition, must faith not have a safety net? What happens when we try to impose one? What boat of security/comfort is He calling you to step out of?

- Are there any areas of your life where you know you would hesitate to trust Jesus? If so, what are your doubts founded on? What words of Jesus do you anchor your faith on?

10

The Fusion of Diversity

I have often stated how precious and unique each one of us is created to be. We live in a world of such diversity and richness; you would think there is nothing we cannot accomplish or achieve as human beings that can benefit the whole of humanity and the whole of creation upon this earth. And yet so often, disunity and conflict rather than harmony and cooperation dominate how we respond to the issues of life.

We can sectarianise and polarise our differences in an endless stream of judgementalism and intolerance of our unique individuality. Could it be we have lost the ability to celebrate one another and instead choose to criticise and condemn, causing factions, schisms and hostile suspicion and scepticism? We continually separate rather than unify our humanity, and yet we are created to be community and to 'love one another' (John 13:34).

In who He was and what He did, Jesus brought about a movement of God as a relational means by which we re-evaluate our values as human beings created by a loving God, bringing reconciliation, restoration and hope over everything that is broken in our lives. He challenges us to redirect our focus and pursue a transformation of thought and action that enables us to fully embrace our uniqueness in Christ as individuals, not only to celebrate one another, but also together to recreate the vison of human endeavour that can know no limit in its potential to thrive in wholeness of life. That need not change because of circumstances around us or experiences we may go through that are out of our control. The call to follow Him is so radically encompassing, it has the capacity to embrace the whole of humanity.

We are a work in progress in our walk with Jesus. It presents daily challenges, particularly in our approach to others. It is here that the attitudes we are called to embrace point to how such a nature is developed in us, when we allow His Spirit to continually draw us closer to the heart of God, affecting our relationships with one another. It is here that compassion for others becomes the driving force in our life responses. But they not only represent our individual reaching out to others in love, but of necessity also require a corporate response that reflects the unity of one body in Christ in its diversity, to direct our corporate mission. God's plan and purpose for each one of us is a collective.

We thrive in the company of others. We are blessed in the fellowship of others, as we in turn bless them. Our wholeness and well-being lie in the hands of those who draw alongside us in encouragement and support. Our vision is enlarged when it is shared and owned by others of likeminded conviction. Our prosperity grows when we give ourselves to one another in the compassionate outworking of our different needs. Our hope lies in that which is common to us all: the desire to love and be loved. We are enriched by difference, not restricted by it.

That is the beauty of how God created us and how He has drawn us together to walk alongside one another in this life. When Jesus calls you to follow Him, know that He also calls others to walk alongside you on that path. This is a model of unity He beckons us to display and live out in witness to a fragmented world that functions by a multi-tier of 'haves and have nots', escalated by endless streams of disjointed differences that further divide us.

Even within developed democracies, we see increased evidence of polarisations within societies and communities that spill over into hostility and violence. The world is not at peace with itself, nor can it be in its current dilemma. So what do you and I, as disciples of Jesus, have to offer?

That we may be one

I have a passion for ecumenical unity in the Church, as does Sheryl. It is such a profound concept, it caused Jesus to pray earnestly to His Father for it as He was coming to the end of His earthly ministry. Why? Because of the impact such a bond of oneness would have upon the world, 'that they all may be one, as You, Father, *are* in Me, and I in You; that they also may be one in Us, that the world may believe that You sent Me' (John 17:21).

I believe there is a growing desire among denominations within the Church for a greater coming together, but it is a large 'institutional vessel' that takes time to change course, rather like a super tanker on the high seas trying to do a U-turn. It is not a sudden about-turn. It takes courage and it takes risk. But above all, it must come about by the move of God's Spirit, because only He can lay on our hearts the conviction needed to step beyond our differences, beyond our centuries of traditional doctrinal boundaries and barriers, and beyond our 'territorial' entrenchments that can at times pay lip service to real unity. Such a move requires us to see the potential we all hold and the unique richness we can each bring.

The litmus test lies in how willing we are to break free from those boundaries and create something radically and dynamically different. How courageous are we to enter such a walk of unity that goes beyond the occasional pulpit exchange, ecumenical gathering as a walk of witness or other infrequent initiatives? Are we desiring to buy into and own such a vision wholesale, where we can acknowledge through our actions that we are the Church of Jesus Christ in this town, that we are one Church? What would such a step take and what would it possibly look like? To begin with, I am not suggesting dismantling our denominational identities and abolishing our institutional frameworks that have centuries of spiritual wealth and development in them. Nor am I suggesting we somehow create a single denomination out of it. I believe that would be both impossible and unnecessary.

The issue is not our denominational variances, but how we can fuse the beauty and diversity into a collective vision that enhances each in its value and contribution to the local mission we are called to, to see a unified kingdom advancement, penetrating our communities with such influential impact as to cause those on the outside to sit up and take notice. It is one thing to evangelise in the town centre with a handful of conscientious disciples. It is something else for that 'handful' to be several hundred witnessing and sharing to those passing through on their way. What impact might that have?

The notion that we, whatever our denominational stance, perceive ourselves to have the right model of Church has always been around. In Capernaum, we see the disciples arguing among themselves as to who would be the greatest, until Jesus pointed out to them that anyone who desired to take first place must put himself last and be a 'servant of all' (Mark 9:33-35). And to make the point stick, He took a 'little child' in His arms, highlighting that their focus must be on even those who are seen as small and insignificant in the world's eyes (Mark 9:36-37). But it did not end there. The sectarian mentality still ensued when John, perhaps somewhat boastfully, informed Jesus that they had earlier seen someone outside their group 'casting out demons in [His] name' (Mark 9:38) and stopped him. Why? Because he was not one of them.

So often there is a reluctance to acknowledge, let alone participate in, a ministry initiated by another church, let alone another denomination. There is almost a conviction among some that it cannot be valid because it is outside their 'jurisdiction', and so we undervalue and diminish the potential impact that can be released. Jesus stopped His disciples in their tracks and instead pointed to something greater and more advantageous. Supposing, rather than criticising, we were to encourage cross-denominational mission.

> But Jesus said, 'Do not forbid him, for no one who works a miracle in My name can soon afterward speak evil of Me. For he who is not against us is on our side. For whoever gives you a cup of water to drink in My name, because you belong to Christ, assuredly, I say to you, he will by no means lose his reward.'
> *Mark 9:39-41*

What I find significant in these remarks Jesus makes is that not only are all those involved in His mission significant and worthy, regardless of whose group they belong to, but they are also to be supported and encouraged. The idea of offering a 'cup of water' can perhaps be viewed as giving help and cooperation across our denominational divides.

If we were to open our eyes to just how much we have to offer one another in a cooperative spirit of working together for His kingdom's sake, to enrich the potential of seeing something significant rise, would that stir in us a passionate enthusiasm for more?

We each have such a wealth of treasure. Let us not throw the baby out with the bathwater because we disagree with what are often secondary issues in what we hold as paramount. The richness and abundance in the 'cup of water' we can offer one another in the pulling together of resources and experiences for a common initiative in missional opportunity could create a dynamic beyond anything we could achieve as individual pockets of church across our cities, towns or villages. We are not in competition with one another, because we are one body, though at times we can act as if we were competing. The fusion of diversity is not uniformity, but collaboratively acknowledging each other's necessity and importance, underpinning it with support and encouragement; even resourcing or strengthening those ministries that have a place in God's purposes and need support to succeed.

When Sheryl and I first came to Braintree and were steered towards visiting all the various churches in the area, we assumed it was initially to find a suitable and appropriate church fellowship where we could settle and worship. The reality that God already had that in hand points to the fact that He had another purpose in it. We came from a ministry where we worked closely with other churches to create something that was all-embracing in the mission of His whole Church in the area. Our One Church initiative built a lot of bridges and strong relationships across the denominational communities in Rainham as well as courting favour in the community, and it was something we were sad to leave behind. But its heart went with us and the passion for engaging with the wider community as the whole people of God remained. It was perhaps unfinished business that stirred a fresh tugging at our heartstrings to engage once again. It was this fire that increasingly rekindled in us as we settled in Braintree.

We love the church we are part of, and especially the people we have become close to in this fellowship. It is an environment that allows God's Spirit to move and release vision. The leadership encourages such opportunities to create new ventures of sharing the good news of Jesus Christ and to embrace those in the community who are open to building relationships. It is here that, among other things, Manor Community was born and has begun to draw all kinds of people together.

There is always more that God wants to do in and through us. It is never an end, but so often a springboard to ever-greater opportunities and developments. Why are we surprised when God calls us to expect more and to climb to greater heights? He is the God who brings the impossible into being. He is the God of surprises who continually raises our bar of expectation.

The nature of following Him is to be open to seeing the new pathways He takes us on, and the places before us. It is here that we are challenged, where the boundaries of our expectations are stretched and we can reimagine new possibilities. This is also the place we are drawn to and to which we draw others whom He calls to walk with us in what He wants to release. It is here we discover that He chooses to blur the denominational boundaries. It is here that real excitement and motivation is released.

Vision is for sharing

So there we were, Sheryl and I, sitting in our garden midsummer, together with our pastor and his wife, sharing afternoon tea. It was a time of limited respite in the pandemic, where small numbers of people could gather outside in gardens and in public places. It was simply an opportunity to spend some time together and enjoy one another's company, but also to share our hearts. I love times like this with people we are close to and can be open with.

God was already stirring in us the desire for creating something in the centre of town that enabled the community to engage with one another, with the Church being at the centre, not dissimilar to the Ship Centre concept at Rainham. The Ship Centre was a community hub, whose multifunctional purpose could embrace a network of people coming together, bringing opportunities and resources through the various community groups and agencies that served the town. Here we could discover community at its best, as a fusion of diversity, where need and provision find a place of belonging.

This is a vision that weaves together a wide circle of stakeholders in partnership who could share these facilities and have ownership of it, giving each an input into its conceptual development, to create a place for gathering people of all walks of life who are part of our community. Families in crisis, those who are homeless, those living with addictions, those who are lonely, isolated or wrestling with mental health issues, to name but a few. A place of befriending and supporting, of directing and equipping, of facilitating and encouraging. A place of working together and sharing space and resources for the benefit of all. A place that is safe and inviting and does not discriminate. A place where loving our community takes on a practical outworking of involvement and building relationships that enrich all our lives; a place of hope, inspiration, direction and reassurance. A place where the love of God in Jesus is tangibly visible.

It was this passion, this vision, that we shared that afternoon in a sun-filled courtyard where we sat together. It led to an invitation to share this at the church leaders' next ecumenical meeting. It was here that a seed was planted among the churches represented. A fire was lit in some, with understandable questions about the practicalities. But this was not about pulling together a string of ideas and suggestions as to a way forward. We believed it was not our idea but God's and, as such, required us to seek His will, His purpose, His strategy and His vision. From our experience at Rainham, it was only when we earnestly spent time with Him and sought His way forward that we were able to step fully into His purposes and see them take shape as He desired.

What did emerge as we shared that initial time together was a picture that helped explain the concept of what could come about. It was like a wheel, the spokes of which spread out in all directions and, at the same time, came together into a central whole. This was the image Sheryl had in her mind while praying for discernment. It was also the image others had at the meeting. But in addition, each spoke on this wheel represented one of the churches in the area. Separately, the spokes could not support any movement of the wheel and it would come apart very quickly, because the weight would cause any individual spoke to collapse. But bound by an outer rim that encompassed and held it all together, that was a whole new ball game.

If that was to be the case here, then our starting point would need to be for us all to come together in prayer and to grow in our relationships with one another before anything else could be accomplished. And this we encouraged. A weekly prayer meeting via Zoom gathered some of the churches as we began to pray and grow closer together. This quickly turned into meeting twice weekly.

It is ongoing. It has no perceived timescale in seeking an outcome. God will not be hurried or cajoled. We believe this is His agenda and His timescale. Its primary purpose at this stage is to bind us in unity, being Christ-centred and kingdom-driven with the focus on His glory. It is a step of recognition of our interdependence and genuine love for one another.

There is biblical precedence. When Joshua took over the leadership of Israel from Moses, as he stood at the edge of the Promised Land, God declared to him:

> Moses My servant is dead. Now therefore, arise, go over this Jordan, you and all this people, to the land which I am giving to them – the children of Israel. Every place that the sole of your foot will tread upon I have given you, as I said to Moses.
> *Joshua 1:2-3*

It is the kind of promise that directs our walk with Him into a future vision shaped by obedient trust in His Word. It is the kind of prophetic word that was given to us at the start of our time in Braintree: the promise of God setting His church on fire, which in turn would ignite the street, the flames of which would lead all the way into the town centre, a town He was going to take. A town He was giving to us.

We believe this is not arrogance or wishful thinking, but divine direction. It has vision and it has purpose. It is about the kingdom of God, His reign and His presence influencing all those who live and work here. It requires courage and risk to step into such a large vision, because such a mission is not for the faint-hearted. Nor is it one that can be accomplished by mere human endeavour or initiative. This is about a move of God that He requires us to step into, because it is a path He has laid before us that we should walk in. It requires a 'faith-filled "**yes**"', but also boldness and fortitude.

To Joshua He said, 'Be strong and of good courage, for to

this people you shall divide as an inheritance the land which I swore to their fathers to give them' (Joshua 1:6). It was a tall order, where twice more God repeated the command to be strong and courageous and obedient to His word in all that was to come about. In this they would be prosperous, because He was going with them and there was no room for being 'afraid [or] dismayed' (Joshua 1:7-9).

Whenever we stand on the edge of something so big, the temptation is understandably to weigh up the odds, and often we base our perception on past experiences of things not quite working out as we would have hoped. We can be daunted by the prospect in front of us, with all the 'what ifs' filling our minds and hearts amid scepticism and doubt. Courage is not required when we are operating from a comfort-zone stance. Risk is not necessary when something is certain or already there. It is when something so seemingly unachievable is presented to us that we must rely totally on cooperating with God to see it fulfilled. We can sometimes stay shy of sharing the good news of Jesus with one person, let alone a whole town, or a whole land, as that which lay before Joshua and his people.

This is a whole-body mission, not an individual enterprise. It requires vision holders who have the passion and the fire to drive the concept forward and put shape to it. But it also requires ownership to enable the vision to be birthed and developed with the support and resourcing of a mobilised Church.

All hands on deck

Not all the tribes of Israel crossed into the Promised Land. For the Reubenites, Gadites and half the tribe of Manasseh, their 'Promised Land' was to settle in the fertile region of Gilead, where their large numbers of livestock would find fertile ground for grazing. It was part of the land conquered by the advancing Israelites on the east bank of the Jordan.[60] They argued with

---

[60] Deuteronomy 3:1-13.

Moses that they should be given this land and settle here, but there was reluctance on his part to allow it, for some obvious reasons.

> And Moses said to the children of Gad and to the children of Reuben: 'Shall your brethren go to war while you sit here? Now why will you discourage the heart of the children of Israel from going over into the land which the LORD has given them?'
> *Numbers 32:6-7*

It was a bit of an affront to the other tribes. They had all got to this stage by their unity as one body to overcome and conquer the land they stood on. Now was not the time to abandon their brothers and say, 'Thanks very much. We're happy here and we'll leave you to it. Hope you get on alright.' It would have been such a discouragement to those crossing, and a divided force would be a greatly weakened force. Bear in mind also, their reputation of defeating the Amorite kings had gone ahead of them across the Jordan and had spread fear among the people and places they were about to invade.[61] Thus, an agreement was struck whereby they would be allowed to settle in Gilead, leaving their women, children and livestock there, on condition that their fighting men would join the rest in battle, and when victory was secured they could return to their settlement.[62] This is what Joshua re-enforced as they were about to cross over and start their campaign of conquest under his leadership.[63] The land would be conquered only by a united Israel. The Lord gave them the land as a unified people; not dispersed. It wasn't designed as an 'every tribe for themselves' mentality or approach, but a whole-body movement. It was in the fusion of their diversity that they would prosper, and only in that place of unity could that come about.

---

[61] Joshua 2:9-11.
[62] Deuteronomy 3:18-20.
[63] Joshua 1:12-15.

We can sometimes have a 'tribal' mentality when it comes to Church, by sticking to our denominational entrenchments of 'parochialism'. In the same way, we can remain disconnected even within our own fellowships, where we go separate ways and do separate things, settling for separate comfort zones that suit our disposition. In such instances, shared vision and missional endeavours are not always owned by the church as a body movement, but compartmentalised within pockets of those who are committed in this way. But we are called to be one, unified in His body, not a confederation of separate islands. Our commitment lies solely in Jesus. He has only one Church, as scattered and diverse as it is. We are the body of Christ, not the bodies of Christ. We are called to be one.

When God indicated that He was 'giving us this town' and setting us and it on fire with a passion, it had a clause in it that was a given: it is the concerted effort of the whole body of Christ here in Braintree that is required to successfully accomplish that which God has ordained. It is in our combined strength that the fullness of His power can be released.

There is a place for our diverse settlements to be invested in – our individual ministries, our missional endeavours and projects, our engagement with community issues and the like. But there is also a time to 'cross over' as one body and one unified movement led by the Spirit of God in advancement of His kingdom.

It is right and proper to maintain our pastoral responsibilities in our local fellowships to build up our people. But the combined gifting of what God wants to release needs to be integrated into a spearheaded initiative of collaboration and vision for bringing the gospel into its full potential. Isn't the Church at its best, at its most powerful and influential, when it embraces this kind of unity? When such a unified love is released, it is unstoppable. It is the very nature of who we are called to be as disciples.

Thought break

- What draws people together when there is a common threat or situation that affects everyone? Do you think we genuinely learn lessons from past experiences? Why/why not?

- How do you handle differences you experience in your church fellowship? Are the things that are common and shared important enough to outweigh the areas of conflict?

- How courageous do you think the Church needs to be to engage with God's mission in a 'secularised' world? What are the risks we need to take to fulfil the commission Jesus gave us in Matthew 28:18-20?

Part 3
The Expectations of Following

11

The Attitude of Being

Whenever we take on a new task, a new job or a new initiative, we set certain expectations to complete or fulfil the purpose or nature of what we undertake. Sometimes, such as from an employer, those expectations are presented to us in the form of job descriptions, rules and regulations, or intended aims and objectives. Many of us are familiar with this sort of contractual requirement, which we may have undertaken at some stage or other. But the expectations here are normally external. They define our performance and outcome within the context of what we bring to the task or project. By and large they are not intended to alter or redefine our identity, or the nature of our character or personality. They operate in the context of who we already are and what we are required to accomplish for those who employ us. The primary purpose or aim here is to achieve the goal set before us.

But what if our call to follow Jesus primarily rests not just on the completion of a mission, but on transforming us in the process; to radically shape our being to become more like the One we are following and, in that sense, to develop into the person we were created to be in all its fullness? Because to accomplish all that Jesus accomplished and commissioned us to continue requires us to take on the full nature of the One to whom we surrender all and for whom we completely live. Our reason for being changes, as does the direction of our lives. Paul stresses this when he writes:

> But what things were gain to me, these I have counted loss for Christ. Yet indeed I also count all things loss for the excellence of the knowledge of Christ Jesus my Lord, for whom I have suffered the loss of all things, and count them as rubbish, that I may gain Christ and be found in Him, not having my own righteousness, which *is* from the law, but that which *is* through faith in Christ, the righteousness which is from God by faith; that I may know Him and the power of His resurrection, and the fellowship of His sufferings, being conformed to His death, if, by any means, I may attain to the resurrection from the dead.
> *Philippians 3:7-11*

The course of Paul's life completely changed when He was confronted by Jesus on that Damascus Road, not only redirecting his whole journey in what lay ahead, but also redefining his purpose and identity. Paul was willing to give up his previous lifestyle for something far more precious than anything he had experienced before. His life had new meaning that spurred him on with passion and zeal, whereby even amid hardship, adversity and life-threatening encounters, the vision and drive that embraced him would not diminish. His aim was to press on to take hold of all that Jesus lay before him when He took hold of Paul, the reward of that 'call of God' he discovered in Jesus (Philippians 3:12,14).

What we gain far outweighs what we lose or surrender in the decision to follow Jesus. Many of us strive in our own strength to accomplish or attain something that is beyond us, or an ideal we aspire to but often fail. I do not for one minute believe we are called to achieve some sort of perfectionist goal, but rather to surrender our will, our thinking and our lifestyle.

God wants us to understand the implications of the choices we make and the expectations of radically shifting our focus when we take on the journey of discipleship. It becomes no longer about us but about Him: His indwelling presence, His visibility in us and His power released through us. Only in a walk of transformation can such an outcome occur, when we seek His will over our own. The nature of such intimacy with Him demands nothing less.

Our lives can often be pressurised with the wrong kind of expectations we place on ourselves or have placed on us by others. They can be unrealistic and demanding, because often they can never be reached, and the harder we try to do so – to be good, to be perfect, to be accepted and the like – the greater the disappointment when we fail to see those traits in ourselves. We try harder and the dissatisfaction grows in an endless cycle of striving and failing and pushing on but missing the mark. Even Christians can be made to feel that they must somehow shine and be morally and ethically above reproach. The pressure to 'perform this religious act' does not enhance their identity in Christ but rather undermines it.

We can all strive for perfection in our lives, and yet we live in an imperfect world and daily are confronted with all kinds of imperfections. There is something in the human psyche, I believe, that drives us towards the 'better' syndrome that perfectionism fuels. It causes us to strive beyond who we are and what we have, always wanting to accomplish or achieve more, which is then reflected in how we live our lives and the things we surround ourselves with.

We are made in the image and likeness of a perfect God, and because we are fallen through sin, we are in conflict within ourselves and continually strive to shake off our imperfections while trying to grasp that which is unspoilt. Our crisis lies in living under this unfulfilled shadow that never sees the light of hope that is brought about through God's redemptive acceptance of us, knowing who we are and who we can become.

Understanding and recognising that we have been redeemed and set free to truly become the person God has called us to be, in every sense of those words, is the starting point that changes our perception of ourselves: 'Stand fast therefore in the liberty by which Christ has made us free, and do not be entangled again with a yoke of bondage' (Galatians 5:1).

I am not suggesting that we should not aim to better ourselves or strive towards ambitions and goals, but our security and confidence, as well as our self-worth and significance, do not lie in our ability to aspire to the notion that God will only accept us if we excel in our lives. He cannot love us any more than He already does.

But neither does He want to leave us where we are. There is potential in every one of us to soar above our immediate capabilities, mindset and attitudes, and that rests in Him, not in ourselves. It is by the empowering Spirit of God living in us that such transformation takes place. It comes as we expose ourselves to God's Word and will. He doesn't call those who are or see themselves as endowed with the ability to fulfil the tasks ahead, but rather equips and infills those whom He has called. The question is whether I desire to change.

Paul draws this out very succinctly when he writes: 'And do not be conformed to this world, but be transformed by the renewing of your mind, that you may prove what *is* that good and acceptable and perfect will of God' (Romans 12:2). What does that imply for you and me?

This is more than just a behavioural issue. It involves our perception, attitude and approach to how we are called to live our lives. It embraces everything about us that directs our outlook, lifestyle and response to whatever life brings our way. But more than that, it invites us to rediscover who it is God has called us to be.

To be conformed to the world in which we live is to accept the patterns of living that are evocative of worldly standards and perceptions that are fickle and constantly in flux. They change with every whim of new thoughts and ideas that emerge and have no real anchorage or foundation. Fleeting and reckless, they throw caution to the wind and feed on self-seeking values driven by all manner of desirable and persuasive pulls that entice and then disappoint. Any aspirations we reach out for or strive towards in an earthly sense can very soon evaporate. We become pulled and pushed about in a labyrinth of illusions and virtual realities that dash our hopes and dreams on the rocks of indifference to our real needs, and we are left as orphans struggling with a myriad of issues that rob us of our true worth and identity. It is an outward false reality that has no inner substance. Its appearance is very enticing and convincing, but so often in life leaves us empty.

That can be our default pattern of thought. But Paul calls us to change how we respond. It is a transformation not just in our minds, but in our will, the very core of our inner being where renewal takes place. It is like pressing the reset button on a computer to restore the original settings and bring it back to the manufacturer's standard. It holds the potential of God's redemptive power to initiate a newness of life in our thinking, our behaviour and our attitudinal approach to every area of our lives. It characterises the values of kingdom living under God's sovereign directive and guidance, as opposed to the futility of our earthly endeavours, however well intended and 'godly' they may appear.

There is a television programme Sheryl and I absolutely love, where people from all around the nation bring precious treasures and heirlooms that are damaged, broken, neglected and in disrepair, having in some cases been like that for decades, passed down from parents, grandparents and even further back. Behind each one lies a heartfelt story and memories that those individuals want to preserve and pass on to the next generation. Expert craftsmen in their field are then assigned to restore these items and return them to their owners in their renewed condition, not only breathing new life into them, but also bringing new hope and joy to those who had all but given up on seeing them as they were before.

The expressions and emotions displayed on the faces of the recipients when these repaired items are presented are priceless. In some cases, a weight that has been carried for many years we see lifted, and the burdens of responsibility removed. To some, these things may seem small and insignificant, but to those people who bring their valued items in trust, restoration means everything.

We do not know what each of us carries or what each one of us has experienced in our lives, nor the burdens that weigh us down. Sometimes we are not even aware ourselves of the nature of the baggage that is uniquely ours, or how to overcome the obstructions that hold us back or press us down, where things in our lives have fallen apart, or been neglected.

Our lives can appear like those items brought to the expert repairers in the hope of them being fixed. Placing them into the hands of the One who can change things in an unprecedented way will bring not only transformation but also renewed hope and purpose, empowering us to live and function as we were intended to; we will then see new life emerge.

Encounter that embraces expectation

I love going to Christian conferences; the buzz and the atmosphere of those huge gatherings, full of anticipation, where engaging in fellowship, worship and teaching is so inspiring and refreshing. I call them the mountaintop experiences, designed to encourage us in the 'valleys' with enthusiasm and motivation to 'go for it' when we return to our normal everyday settings.

I come back fired up and excited at the prospects ahead. They are occasions of richness in the unfolding of the Word of God, shared by many and various divinely inspired and gifted speakers. I always want to glean from them all those pearls of wisdom and insights. I often hang on every word, writing copious notes in the process. Their delivery is never long enough for me. I sit there at the end of the talks wanting more.

I recall the first time we, as a family, went to Spring Harvest at Easter. We were in a dry place and desperately needing the experience this occasion gave us. We had never been anywhere like it, and the newness and vibrancy on every level was something we treasure to this day. It was a safe environment for our young children, too, who also benefited from the experience: they had freedom to engage with their peers in exciting new ways, with biblical teaching and worship and other activities, just as we, the adults, did.

When we travelled home at the end of the week, we were in tears, because none of us wanted to leave. We encouraged others from our church fellowship to join us the following year, and after that the numbers continually increased, as they did with other conferences we attended.

Imagine how much more of an encounter it would have been to be among the crowds who followed Jesus as He sat down on the mountainside and began to teach the growing swell, His disciples among them, waiting and hanging on every word He uttered. We read about the Sermon on the Mount in chapters 5 to 7 of Matthew's Gospel; Jesus' profound teaching has sent echoes down the centuries in its challenging and transformational wisdom, with far-reaching consequences.

It is challenging because here Jesus sets out, I believe, the expectations of what it means to follow Him, to become like Him in the characteristics of kingdom living, and what that looks like. It is transformational because in this teaching we see the necessity for a mind shift in our attitude and the prerequisite for a lifestyle that is radically different from that of a worldly nature.

What was being unfolded was uncompromising in its approach and thinking regarding every aspect of our lives as followers of Christ. Its impact left His audience amazed and stunned.

> And so it was, when Jesus had ended these sayings, that the people were astonished at His teaching, for He taught them as one having authority, and not as the scribes.
> *Matthew 7:28-29*

Just pause for a moment and think on this question: what expectations of living does the world place on you, and who does the world say you should be?

It's not a straightforward question, nor is the answer simple. There are so many values and truths emerging every day; each, in the world's eyes, as valid as the next. Some expectations contradict others. Some are incomprehensible and even outlandish. Some are common sense. But in this world, we all live by a myriad of interpretations of what life should look like, what is acceptable or not, and even that changes across generations and within them.

So where do we even begin to explore the reality of how our lives should function as people created in love to be love? And in any case, whose love are we to emulate or aspire to? Perhaps the truth lies not out there but within, in the very core of who we are, reflecting not an outward standard but one that needs to be inherent in us, directed by the One who created us and calls us to renewal in Him.

What makes us, as followers of Jesus, different from everyone else? It is here that Jesus begins to unfold the expectations that transformation brings to us, profoundly challenging our assumptions of acceptable lifestyles in the realm of the King.

Blessedness has purpose

When at the start of this sermon we look at those Jesus describes as being 'blessed' (Matthew 5:3-12), there are several things to consider. What do you think it means to be blessed? It is our practice, when we come to the end of the day, for Sheryl and me to recollect all the blessings we have encountered that day, and then to give thanks to God for His goodness to us in them. It is often surprising how many we recall.

There are many ways in our lives that blessings can occur. We can be blessed with good health, firm friendships and stable family life, contentment at work or other areas of our life, and so on. I wonder if, when Jesus began this sermon, as He sat down to address the crowds, He had another focus for the word 'blessed'. I suggest it portrays an attitude of inner reality that generates an external response.

These 'attitudes of being' relate to who we are in Christ, anchored in His love and grace. We are immersed into the nature of who He is, affecting every area of our lives, encapsulating a kingdom lifestyle with Him. They point not to living in this world with an earthly perspective, but to the eternal realm of His kingdom, where our approach to life is quite different.

Jesus unfolds the attitude and mindset of the true follower who is committed to that transformational walk. This is the best way of life (of being blessed) not only in its goodness, but also in its results. It is here, embraced in a right relationship with Him, that Jesus calls us blessed, because it is here that we experience the full nature of His empowerment in us. This is where our expectations lie, carrying with it satisfaction and favour, bringing joy and contented happiness, knowing it is not our circumstances that dictate who we are, but God Himself who edifies, encourages and empowers us in that blessing. It encompasses a sense of holiness and being set apart for His purposes and gives us reassurance of all we press into in our discipleship. It gives us the security and foundation in our lives that reflect who we are as overcomers.[64]

It is this blessedness that in many ways is a gift that brings with it eternal rewards and is therefore a walk that is not in vain, but one that progressively shapes us to be all we are created to be, reflecting in us the nature of Jesus' compassion for His lost world, because it is anchored in Him. It is a message that speaks of humility and commitment to brotherly love, the expectation that lies at the heart of kingdom living. Its aim was not to rewrite the commandments as an external edict but to imbed in us the need to change the inner person. In this context, love becomes the primary motivation. But what does that involve and what are its implications? It is here that we see the treasures of this

---

[64] Romans 8:37; Revelation 3:21.

sermon released.

First, we need to realise that our perspective on life is not like God's.[65] He sees way beyond our understanding of what is right, beneficial and fruitful for our well-being. And He always has our best interests at heart. Remember, Jesus came to show us the depth of God's love for us. But we also need to comprehend that in a broken and sinful world, love is costly, because His kingdom ways are not the world's ways, and His light has come to break into our darkness and set us free from the tyranny of sin.[66] Love is the currency with which this is achieved.

Second, love is the driving force of everything God has done because He 'is love' (1 John 4:16,19). As disciples of Jesus, we are called to respond to His love and, as such, to embrace and reflect that love to others.[67] Such love must be all-consuming. Compassion for others must be the driving force that fuels our response in reaching out to people, because it was Jesus' response.[68]

It involves the willingness to give up everything and surrender all, to reach out to those who are lost. That is a tall order, some would say. Yes, it is, because life matters; people matter: they matter to God and are precious to Him. But it is also a matter of knowing that we cannot achieve it ourselves in our own strength. Only Jesus can, and therefore only in Him do we truly discover the 'treasure' we are to others (2 Corinthians 4:7).

It is in the selfless giving of ourselves that we truly discover our impact and worth to others. That is why we are called 'blessed' when we obey the call of Jesus to follow. If we are serious about His agenda for us, it requires self-denial in abandoning our attachments to earthly things and securities and to 'take up [our] cross' – being prepared to suffer and be rejected

---

[65] Isaiah 55:8-9.
[66] John 3:19-21; John 10:10.
[67] John 15:17.
[68] Matthew 9:36.

for His sake and the sake of His kingdom (Mark 8:34).

Only in this way can we truly and 'fruitfully' follow where He leads and see lives transformed through His power. It is the power of self-giving love that accomplishes this through Him who paid the ultimate price on the cross. This is where we begin, as we explore all the unfolding truth Jesus teaches here in this mountain setting.

Thought break

- Reflect for a moment on the things that you count as blessings in your life. Are these blessings any different from those who do not profess a relationship with Jesus? If so, in what way?

- What do you admire most in people who are committed in their discipleship and reflect that in their lifestyle?

- What are your expectations in life? How different do you think they might be from the expectations God has for you? Can the two be aligned, and if so, how?

12

Foundational Hallmarks

The poor in spirit, those who mourn, the meek

Most of us may be familiar with the term 'born again', in whatever way we choose to define it. But what does the term imply? It is, I believe, first and foremost to enter a personal relationship with Jesus and experience a process of transformation that radically changes our thinking and acting. All we hold as the norm needs to be redirected into a kingdom-centred mindset. As followers of Jesus, we cannot release the kingdom of God unless we are in the kingdom of God.

A Pharisee named Nicodemus was troubled with niggling thoughts and questions. I suspect this devout Jewish ruler was being challenged by what he heard and saw in Jesus. Eventually he succumbed to his inquisitive spirit and, out of sight of his peers, paid Jesus a visit in secret: 'This man came to Jesus by night and said to Him, "Rabbi, we know that You are a teacher come from God; for no one can do these signs that You do unless God is with him"' (John 3:2). And so a discourse ensues whereby Nicodemus is challenged in his thinking. How would he respond to the demands Jesus spelt out when it comes to following Him? 'Jesus answered and said to him, "Most assuredly, I say to you, unless one is born again, he cannot see the kingdom of God'" (John 3:3).

I'm not sure if Nicodemus was simply naïve when he questioned how someone can be physically born again from the same womb,[69] or if he was feeling somewhat uncomfortable with the implication of what Jesus was intimating and therefore tried to divert where this was going by a pointless response. Jesus didn't give that question any airtime, but merely pressed in by deepening what He had already said:

> Jesus answered, 'Most assuredly, I say to you, unless one is born of water and the Spirit, he cannot enter the kingdom of God. That which is born of the flesh is flesh, and that which is born of the Spirit is spirit. Do not marvel that I said to you, "You must be born again."'
> John 3:5-7

To be transformed in this way is essential if anyone is to begin to grasp (see) or engage with (enter) a kingdom lifestyle whereby God's reign and realm are manifestly evident in that person's life. How do you differentiate between a born-again approach to relationship with God and a nominal religious observance that appears on the surface as genuine but has little or no impact on either that person's lifestyle or their influence and witness to others?

When we submit our lives to Christ, it is this relational walk with God that governs our motives, our aspirations, our purpose and the direction our lives take in pursuing Him: 'The wind blows where it wishes, and you hear the sound of it, but cannot tell where it comes from and where it goes. So is everyone who is born of the Spirit' (John 3:8).

It is not easily understood by someone who has not yet experienced that encounter with God in Jesus Christ. Like the wind, we see its effects but beyond that, outwardly, there is little comprehension of the spiritual dimension that embraces and transforms everything about us. This is something Nicodemus,

---

[69] John 3:4.

with all his intellectual religious knowledge and experience, struggled to comprehend.

Being born again, by its very nature, is a process and not just a decision; it is a journey that is reflected in the kingdom values that shape our inner being, where our attitudes, approaches and responses to life's issues and encounters are grounded and underpinned. It embraces everything we are transformed to be when we surrender our lives to God. It is an ongoing experience that begins when we say, 'Yes.'

These are the areas of our lives I believe Jesus addresses in this sermon in Matthew 5 to 7; not just in the Beatitudes at the start, but in the whole discourse He presents to His listeners. Every area He touches upon re-enforces the whole, and each profound truth, while acting as a 'stand-alone' pearl, affects and drives home the significance of how as disciples we are called to live our lives with the benefits such an expected lifestyle involves.

The poor in spirit, the mourners, the meek, the hungry for righteousness, the merciful, the pure in heart, the peacemakers and the persecuted are not, I believe, a list of people groups or types of discipleship any more than the fruit of the Spirit of 'love, joy, peace, longsuffering, kindness, goodness, faithfulness, gentleness, self-control' (Galatians 5:22-23) are a list of different character traits to be chosen from. Both are one, and integral to whom we are called to be. They each address the nature and attributes necessary for seeing the reality of kingdom living and being Christ-centred disciples, whose hearts of compassion reflect that of God Himself. This is surely what is expected of those who commit their lives to Him.

If our walk with God embraces a necessity for intimacy with and reliance upon the One we follow in everything our relationship with Him calls us to, then these attributes become the foundational hallmarks that underpin such a path of discipleship. They become our identity because they manifest His.

Compassionate humility

Understanding the part that humility plays in our attitude is where we start, because it reflects how we are connected to God. Humbling yourself before God is not belittling who you are but acknowledging who He is. It is a recognition that we are totally reliant on God for every area of our lives: the very air that we breathe, the very ground we walk on, the ministry and mission we are entrusted with.

Many entrepreneurs rise to great heights of worldly success by an unflinching belief in themselves and what they can achieve, often with a ruthless, competitive streak. And the world applauds them. But humility is not an inferior mindset when it comes to achieving or accomplishing great things. Rather, it recognises that everything comes from and belongs to God.

This is the nature of being 'poor in spirit' (Matthew 5:3). It is not our mission but His. Always was, always will be. When we come to terms with that understanding,, we enable ourselves in true humility to trust in God's provision and direction in guiding and governing our decisions and responses. Like a small child totally dependent upon their parents for everything, we rest in that assurance and knowledge without fear or anxiety.

Such humility is essential in the kingdom of God because if we are not careful, and however well intentioned our motives may be, self-centred agendas and ambitions can very easily redirect and misguide our attention and cause us to wander from the true desires of God's plans and purposes for us. We then find ourselves not only working where He is not, but also putting all our human energies and resources into ministries that are fruitless and even empty.

It is the poor in spirit to whom God releases the resources of heaven and to whom the kingdom of heaven belongs, because we can be entrusted with their implementation, knowing that the glory belongs not to us, but to God Himself. We then want to see His kingdom advanced in our communities, His will released in our lives and His name honoured and made known.

If such humility gives us a starting point, then we can be confident that God will share not only His resources but His heart also. It is here that mourning is addressed by Jesus. To mourn is to grieve for what is lost, to be broken-hearted. Mourning therefore affects our hearts, because it is in this context that our hearts are engaged and where we are touched and affected by the things that break God's heart.

Here His heart influences and changes us by releasing His compassion for the lost; a lost and broken world that has rejected His love and pursues its own self-centred desires and agendas, causing division and separation from the only source that can bring wholeness and well-being to humanity. Jesus, when He looked on Jerusalem and saw the fate of those who rejected Him, wept bitterly over the city, a city and a world He was soon to die for.[70]

Similarly, Jesus wept at the grave of His friend Lazarus. But was He merely grieving for the loss of His friend? I don't think so. When Mary and Martha, Lazarus' sisters, in a state of panic, sent word to Jesus urging Him to come quickly because their brother was seriously ill, Jesus responded in a way they didn't expect. It may have come across as somewhat unsympathetic and harsh because He didn't come rushing back to them: 'When Jesus heard *that*, He said, "This sickness is not unto death, but for the glory of God, that the Son of God may be glorified through it"' (John 11:4). But then, curiously it seems to me, His comment to His disciples indicates clearly that Lazarus has died: 'Then Jesus said to them plainly, 'Lazarus is dead. And I am glad for your sakes that I was not there, that you may believe. Nevertheless let us go to him"' (John 11:14-15).

So what's going on here, because by the time Jesus gets there, Lazarus is already buried four days? Martha in her grief expresses disappointment, because they were sure, had Jesus arrived sooner, He could have prevented His friend's death.

---

[70] Luke 19:41-44.

Their perception was still that of Jesus as a healer, but He would now shift their whole experience of their understanding of Him to another level. He didn't come to heal Lazarus but to raise him from the dead.

They knew their theology regarding resurrection on the last day, but Jesus was going to bring that reality into the present, right before them:

> Jesus said to her, 'I am the resurrection and the life. He who believes in Me, though he may die, he shall live. And whoever lives and believes in Me shall never die. Do you believe this?'
> *John 11:25-26*

Do we believe this today? The theory may work in our heads, but we need to experience and encounter its profound reality to grasp the significance of who Jesus is and what He is calling us to walk in. Jesus came to raise Lazarus from the dead, not to heal him.

I wonder where our own expectations lie regarding some of the challenging life issues that we face. I wonder if we place limitations in those expectations of what we anticipate God can or will do. He has no limitations other than perhaps those our doubts place upon Him.

Jesus came to this situation with purpose and intent, whether people there realised it or not. He already knew what He was going to do as He approached the tomb, yet as He drew near, He wept. Why would He weep for His friend whom He was about to bring back to life? This was no wishful thinking on His part, nor a plea that maybe, fingers crossed, God might somehow bring this about. It was bold and it was confident, with no hesitation. It was intentional.

We can often approach the throne of God's grace with uncertainty and hesitancy, praying sometimes with the added appendage that if it were His will, maybe God would act as we would hope. There was no such uncertainty in Jesus.

He told them to remove the stone. They did, cautiously, but

not before Martha reminded Jesus of the stench that would follow from a four-day-old corpse. The people who gathered around the tomb would have had no idea what was about to happen, nor would they have made the connection with what Jesus had just said to them: 'Did I not say to you that if you would believe you would see the glory of God?' (John 11:40).

We can imagine their distraught and bewildered gazes and the expressions on their faces, demonstrating just how much it was going over their heads. And then, everything came to light.

> Then they took away the stone *from the place* where the dead man was lying. And Jesus lifted up *His* eyes and said, 'Father, I thank You that You have heard Me. And I know that You always hear Me, but because of the people who are standing by I said *this*, that they may believe that You sent Me.' Now when He had said these things, He cried with a loud voice, 'Lazarus, come forth!'
> *John 11:41-43*

And he did!

So, all that said, why did Jesus weep beforehand? Partly to draw alongside those who were grieving, yes. But I would suggest He was not so much mourning for His friend, but rather for the state of the human condition that was so lost in its fallen despair that there was resignation and abandonment to what was perceived as impossible or inevitable.

Sin has such a grip on humanity that hopelessness and despair often cloud our understanding of who God is. Our lack of anticipation and expectation of what He can do diminishes our ability to rise above the limitations we see before us, and we lose the confidence to step out into the kingdom perspective that demands heaven's response.

His weeping and 'groaning in Himself' (John 11:35,38) I believe embraced a righteous anger at the state the carnage of sin has left humanity in. That which was made in His image and likeness to reflect His glory was instead left in despair and anguish, lost and frightened in an uncertain future, where death was the only perceived certainty.

Jesus didn't ask His Father if He might breathe new life into Lazarus. He thanked Him for doing so even before it happened. That's not arrogance but relational intimacy. Like Jesus, we are called to walk from a place of confidently knowing what's on the Father's heart and how He wants us to respond.

Imagine, for example, being called to visit a couple you find distraught and in tears, where a succession of miscarriages has left them beside themselves with grief and despair. They so greatly want to have a family, yet experience only disappointment time after time.

You get alongside them, listen to their story and cry with them, feeling their pain as if it were your own. They are happy for you to pray with them for God to intervene and bring hope into their lives. You pray for the miracle with the conviction that this is on God's heart. In answer to that prayer, a baby is conceived, and you walk with them through this next pregnancy every step of the way, through every scan and every maternity appointment. Their miracle child is born healthy, turning their tears of sadness to rivers of overwhelming joy.

Or imagine perhaps visiting a terminally ill friend in hospital, semiconscious and gasping for their last breath, and as you pray over them with a bold conviction, you see a vision of a transparent canopy covering them and a bright light under it enveloping them from head to toe. You then receive news the very next day that they have made significant recovery and within a few days they are discharged from hospital and their health restored with a new lease of life extended to them.

These examples are based on real events, but I have omitted details to protect identities. These are touching points, where ordinary and extraordinary meet, where the impossible becomes possible and the unimaginable becomes reality. I believe such miracles are happening all the time when heaven is released to touch the earth in life-changing ways that defy our perceived logical understanding.

Mourning is not bowing to the inevitable but being driven

by it to release a kingdom response. When we understand that, what follows is merely the execution of what has already been ordained. Jesus' tears were those of compassion for the human condition enslaved by sin.

It is that compassion, that cry of the heart, which ultimately led Jesus to the cross, where He completely disarmed the powers of darkness that prevailed over the human state. And it is that compassionate heart we are called to walk in, drawing alongside those who are lost and broken. But to have such a heart, we must also recognise the place and condition of brokenness we have come from when we ourselves were lost.

There is something very fulfilling and satisfying when we can serve others in a way that brings hope, relief, support and encouragement to them; when we walk with them through their pain and suffering. But even more so when that also leads them to find the love of God and draws them from a place of darkness and into God's light, transforming their reality in the process.

I believe it is here we find that our comfort and encouragement in God's salvation far outweigh the sacrifice we have had to make in the process. It is here that those who mourn are comforted and encouraged.

Visible community

Humility and compassion direct our approach and response. Who we are and how others perceive us is centred on the nature of our lifestyle. When we are seen as different in a way that is inviting and draws people's inquisitiveness to us because of the love that is visibly seen or demonstrated, it causes a reaction.

That can be positive or negative. It can draw others closer, or it can repel, but it never leaves people indifferent; or at least, it shouldn't. We are called to be influencers in the world, not to be influenced by it. Being accepted or rejected is not the issue. Being visible as a follower of Jesus, in all its empowering impact, is.

The influence Jesus had on those around Him is undeniable. The influence you have on those around you should be too. In essence, what is inside you is revealed by what you release from within you. Jesus describes our visibility by applying the images of salt and light.[71]

Have you ever noticed, looking at the Gospel accounts, the amount of time recorded that Jesus spent in the community as He travelled around, compared with the time spent in the synagogues (not that this didn't matter)? His mission was to engage with humanity, not religion; with the condition of humanity's sinful predicament, not the ritual of their worship and legalism. People were his priority. They were and are what matters to God. It's why Jesus came: to bring hope and purpose, meaning and direction; to restore people's worth and value.

He did not come to condemn but to save those who are lost.[72] It is why so many flocked to Him. He had time for them.[73] Some people think that because God loves us, He accepts us as we are and then they use that as an excuse for living as they please. But that is a false assumption to make. Yes, God does love us, wholeheartedly and enough to send His Son to die for us. But He loves us too much to leave us in the condition we are in when we are enshrouded in sin. He came to bring transformation to our lives, and the Gospels are full of encounters of the changed lives of those with whom He engaged. He is the light that breaks into our darkness.

Jesus calls His disciples to have that same passion for people He has, and to engage with our communities as He did. We are called to be salt and light for a reason. In a world of high technology, we may be forgiven for not appreciating the importance and significance of the necessity for salt and light in our everyday lives.

Our outward physical existence is not the issue, nor our material worldly necessities of life. It is our inner being, our core

---

[71] Matthew 5:13-16.
[72] John 3:17.
[73] Matthew 9:36.

values that define who we really are. Whether we are surrounded by material wealth and comfort or impoverished in squalor, our moral and ethical compass is what directs our thinking and acting. But if that compass is dysfunctional, then so will the path we travel on be.

'You are the salt of the earth; but if the salt loses its flavor, how shall it be seasoned? It is then good for nothing but to be thrown out and trampled underfoot by men' (Matthew 5:13). In the rabbinic traditions of Jesus' time, salt was often used as an image of wisdom. As salt of the earth, divine wisdom should govern our engagement in preserving and directing the fabric of our communities, our society and the foundational framework of our relationships.

Jesus was never afraid to challenge the status quo, and nor should we be. If we fail to speak out and challenge misguided, mistaken or misconceived beliefs and behavioural practices, or corrupt and rebellious attitudes that are contrary to that which God has ordained, then our society, and the communities within, will remain lost in sinful ignorance of the truth.

As such, our influence (flavour) will have no impact and will remain good for nothing. We will become invisible by our own failure to respond to the move of God's Spirit in us, leading and urging us to act and minister to others.

By condoning or accepting the brokenness of fallen moral or ethical standards, and not addressing the presenting issues that confront us, we have nothing to say that makes us as followers of Jesus distinctively countercultural, and instead we are perceived as foolish and irrelevant with little or no impact upon the lives of others. Our faith and witness, like salt, is then trampled on.

We are called to direct others to the God who inspires us. Many churches have vision or mission statements on their noticeboards and placards, such as 'Making Jesus known', and the like. At Rainham, we were no different. Ours was 'Putting the community in touch with Jesus'. It gave us a yardstick to measure our impact in the community by, but unless we reflected that in who we were and how visible we appeared, they remained only slogan words with little significance to those outside.

Our statement of intent must carry our DNA, the reason why we are here. It must underpin everything we are, in and to the community around us. These statements must speak of who we are, not what we aim to be or seek to promote. They are not there to remind us of our identity in Christ and His mission to the community; that should be a given. They are displayed to enable others to understand what we are about, and if they recognise that in us, it will draw them to come closer, because they will have experienced its impact upon the community.

In the same context, we are called to be the light of the world, just as Jesus is the light of the world (John 8:12). 'You are the light of the world. A city that is set on a hill cannot be hidden. Nor do they light a lamp and put it under a basket, but on a lampstand, and it gives light to all *who are* in the house' (Matthew 5:14, 15). Light, like salt, affects its environment by being distinctive. 'Let your light so shine before men, that they may see your good works and glorify your Father in heaven' (Matthew 5:16). By its very nature, light casts out darkness.

Walk into a dark room and switch the lights on. It is no longer dark. In the same way, as light bearers, we are called to change the environment we walk into. If, in Jesus, we stand on holy ground, then every step we take forward should become holy ground.[74] The follower of Jesus who is visibly different will influence others. That may be positively or negatively, but their presence will change the atmosphere because of the presence of Jesus they carry. Paul explains it like this:

> Now thanks *be* to God who always leads us in triumph in Christ, and through us diffuses the fragrance of His knowledge in every place. For we are to God the fragrance of Christ among those who are being saved and among those who are perishing. To the one *we are*

---

[74] 1 Peter 1:15-16.

> the aroma of death *leading* to death, and to the other the aroma of life *leading* to life. And who *is* sufficient for these things?
> *2 Corinthians 2:14-16*

I know I'm mixing metaphors a bit here between light and aroma, but in Jesus they are interchangeable because both carry the idea of influential impact upon others, who necessarily will react one way or the other. Going back to the notion of the dark room which is suddenly lit up, a person standing in that place might hide their eyes because of the sudden brightness, or pleasingly say, 'That's better. I can see now.'

Jesus, who is the 'light of the world', says to His disciples, 'You are the light of the world. A city that is set on a hill cannot be hidden. Nor do they light a lamp and put it under a basket, but on a lampstand, and it gives light to all *who are* in the house' (Matthew 5:14-15).

Some would say faith is a private thing. But a 'secret disciple' who is invisible and, like the lamp, hidden under a basket, is no more use in the world than one who has lost his distinctiveness as salt.

Whether we are called to be visible and influential to a whole community (city) or to individuals (house), the intent is the same. Light by its very nature shines. We are called to shine. Notice light shines best in dark places. That's where it is seen most powerfully. That's where it is clearly visible.

To be light in dark places is to bring positivity into negative environments; to bring reconciliation into division, hope into despair, direction into lost situations and circumstances, love into hatred, comfort into loneliness and grief, healing into brokenness. We are called to turn the atmosphere around us on its head.

When we mourn for the lost and have compassionate hearts that cry out to God, it is then our light is summoned to shine into the broken places we are drawn to, bringing enlightenment and hope.

Meek is not weak

Jesus' lifestyle ensued from a close walk with His Father, resulting in the confidence of knowing who He was and what His purpose was here on earth. It was visible in the inner peace and self-control in which He walked. Self-control is the nature of meekness that Jesus speaks of in His sermon, as those who will 'inherit the earth' (Matthew 5:5).

That may sound strange in a world view where power and brute force are seen as ruling the day, and where dominance is measured by supremacy, not gentleness or meekness. However, meekness is not weakness, but rather inner strength.

When we know who we are in Christ, we have no need or desire to arrogantly presume we are superior to others. Especially among Christians it is indefensible to assume an attitude of being more important than others, perhaps because of our gifting, ministry or status.

There is no such thing as a first-class or second-class Christian, nor for that matter is there such a thing as a first- or second-class human being, even when the world decrees otherwise in various forms. We are equally loved by God and each one of us matters to Him in no undiminished way.

I am always amazed at the way Jesus appeared never to be fazed by any external pressure, accusation or threat. His inner strength and inner peace enabled Him to be measured in every response He made. His reaction to situations was always filled with wisdom and insight that often left his assailants bewildered and spellbound, unable to counter Him in any effective way.

He knew who He was and what He came for. He didn't need to prove anything to anyone. He needed no force of influence or publicity stunts to draw Himself to people's attention. His integrity spoke for itself. His self-control was visibly evident for all to see, as was His submission to His Father's will.

He needed no vindication or flaunting of power or authority, and this freed Him to not only be Himself, but also to exert the kind of influence that changed lives and drew others to Him. It is this kind of meekness that carries inheritance with it because its impact sends ripples across its path, across every area of community.

Those who carry such an attitude find themselves being influential among those around them. The meek are simply those who lean into God for their strength and in submission and trust rely on His will and purpose, rather than seeking praise or glory for themselves.

How we respond to circumstances around us and the situations that press in and provoke us to react negatively or defensively should be anchored in self-control through knowing who we are. Here, as we lean in to God's indwelling presence, we may find our reaction to be more positive and constructive.

We may feel intimidated, but it is our measured and compassionate outworking of love that disarms the onslaughts that seek violence and accusation. Meekness is not disempowerment, but empowerment, knowing where our true inheritance lies: 'But I say to you, love your enemies, bless those who curse you, do good to those who hate you, and pray for those who spitefully use you and persecute you' (Matthew 5:44).

One of the most challenging areas we can experience in conflicts is found in how we react. Our earthly or worldly response is to 'give as good as we get' or to seek revenge on those who have hurt us or opposed us. This is the natural response of a fallen world. If someone hits me, I hit them back; if someone attacks me verbally, I lash out at them. In doing so, we enter a cycle of vendettas, each time upping the stakes and fuelling more hatred and resentment, even rage.

It creates in our spirit something very corrosive and is at the heart of what leads to prejudices, racial tensions and cultural barriers. Its purpose has its roots in evil,[75] aimed to create division in relationships, that destroys our well-being and wholeness; our *shalom*. Jesus very clearly highlights the response we are called to make:

---

[75] Ephesians 6:12.

> You have heard that it was said, 'An eye for an eye and a tooth for a tooth.' But I tell you not to resist an evil person. But whoever slaps you on your right cheek, turn the other to him also. If anyone wants to sue you and take away your tunic, let him have *your* cloak also. And whoever compels you to go one mile, go with him two.
> *Matthew 5:38-41*

Jesus makes no bones about this issue and leaves no room for compromise. But this is not a response made in weakness, intimidation or fear, but rather self-control. How? Violence and aggression are designed to create a reaction of like for like, thus fuelling further violence and aggression. There is a saying: 'It takes two hands to clap.'

When we refuse to jump on the bandwagon of responding in this negative way, and instead seek to defuse the situation with calmness and composure, the conflict quickly evaporates because it is no longer fuelled with the rhetoric of further provocation.

That does not mean we should allow ourselves to be treated as doormats for people to walk all over us. Meekness is not submission in the sense of having no voice or control, leaving us at the mercy of whatever onslaught follows. Quite the opposite. Jesus is not suggesting non-response but rather a kingdom-centred response.

Endured suffering without retaliation has the power to overcome evil and nullify its venom. We see this often in peaceful mass protests opposed to tyrannical regimes, whereby protesters do not succumb to responding with violence to provocation by brutal forces, despite having to endure vicious attacks aimed at crushing their spirit.

Jesus was never out of control nor subservient to the whims of evil intent, even when facing the cross:

> Therefore My Father loves Me, because I lay down My life that I may take it again. No one takes it from Me, but I lay it down of Myself. I have power to lay it down, and

> I have power to take it again. This command I have received from My Father.
> *John 10:17-18*

To effectively reject the need for retaliation, we must put our absolute trust and assured confidence in God, and allow the inner strength He gives to direct the right response. Jesus here is not making some ideological statement, unaware or naïve about the realities of a sinful world that lives in tyranny through sin. His address, remember, is directed at the attitude of those who would follow Him and their approach to the relationships that have their roots in the kingdom of God.

Jesus went silently to the cross, but not passively. He went willingly to overcome, once and for all, the grip that evil had over humankind, defeating the power of sin and death. It is in His sacrificial suffering of total surrender that evil is vanquished and its powers annulled, while, in the process, we are reconciled us to the God of love.[76]

The kind of self-control expected of us is far from easy, because our natural inclination is to demand justice. We know our rights! We want to cling to those rights when they are impinged upon, and we can become very vociferous about it. But in so doing, we do not fully allow Jesus' lordship to reign over us and, as such, we cease to be effective in the power of our witness. We recall in the Beatitudes that the meek are blessed; those whose inner strength and internal peace is not eroded by external influences seeking to rob us of the joy set before us.[77]

Our submission is to God alone. Self-control is part of the fruit of the Spirit, enabling us not only to overcome the insults and hatred direct towards us but also to witness to the power of divine love residing in us, that the world neither knows nor understands. It's. This is where our inheritance lies.[78]

---

[76] Isaiah 53:7; Colossians 2:14,15; Romans 5:8-10.
[77] Hebrews 12:1-2.
[78] John 14:17.

Thought break

- What makes you, as a follower of Jesus, different from everyone else? Would you describe yourself as 'shining bright and salty', or inconspicuous and ineffective in your discipleship? What would those who know you say?

- How do you react to the issues or values people hold that conflict with kingdom values or scriptural teaching? How affected are you in your spirit by issues of sin and brokenness in our society? Have you ever cried for someone who is 'lost'?

- How do you deal with conflict? How evident is self-control in your life?

13

Yearning for More

Those who hunger and thirst for righteousness, the merciful

What do you hunger for? I suspect there are many things that would come up if we were to take a survey. Everything from personal ambitions and life goals to accumulation of wealth, status, power, contentment and whatever else the human heart desires and strives for.

Hunger is a powerful driving force in our lives. It alerts us to something that is lacking, without which we are not satisfied, and so we become preoccupied and even obsessed until our needs are met. That can be positive or negative. But I wonder if righteousness would be among that list of hungers in us.

Certainly, for the disciple of Jesus, it is integral to their identity. We are to 'hunger and thirst for righteousness' (Matthew 5:6). We are to pursue righteousness until we are satisfied, which will only happen when righteousness has been attained. So what are we looking at here?

Righteousness at its basic level is about standing right; not in the sense of being correct, so much as being morally and ethically sound. But standing right according to whom? There are many people groups who would deem their ethical and moral uprightness to be appropriate, while other groups may consider that questionable. In addition, our cultural identity may well play a significant part in what we hold to be acceptable and even commendable.

But what kind of righteousness is Jesus referring to when He calls those who hunger and thirst for it as being blessed and being filled? The righteousness we are considering here is one that is born of God. In other words, being right in God's eyes and measured by His standard of what our lifestyle should look like and be deemed acceptable to Him, because righteousness is one of His attributes. For that very reason we hit a stumbling block, because no one can reach such a high watermark of acceptance when it comes to righteousness.

That said, Jesus encourages us to hunger and thirst for it and therefore it must be attainable. Yes, it is, but only through Him. He is our righteousness, because He chose us and made us right with Him through His shed blood. When we enter that right relationship with Him, Jesus enables us by His Spirit to share in His nature and become the person He created us to be and intends us to grow into. 'For He made Him who knew no sin *to be* sin for us, that we might become the righteousness of God in Him' (2 Corinthians 5:21).

Before I surrendered my life to Jesus, my sights were set on many different things, none of them God-centred. I went in pursuit of the things that were right for me as I perceived them. It was my agenda, my terms and my decisions. It was not driven by any moral compass, necessarily, nor, if I am honest, by any genuine care for others. It was often a self-seeking agenda. That is the nature of a self-absorbed lifestyle. But when we submit our lives to Christ, something shifts. Our desires shift. My desires shifted, as did my priorities. I became hungry and thirsty for something else, something outside my own self-importance. It became a yearning for going deeper into the heart of God in my relationship with Him.

The closer we get, the more that hunger and thirst increases, because we become progressively more aware of the Father's heart, longing that others should come into a right relationship with Him and experience His life-changing love for themselves. There comes a growing dissatisfaction with a worldly status quo, where the name of God is at best tolerated, but increasingly ignored, or blasphemed, and His ways rejected and even reviled. It is this rejection of His truth that makes our hearts cry out, eager that others would see and turn to Him.

This is the nature of our righteousness in Christ. Righteousness is active. God looked on a broken and sin-drenched world and acted to change that. When we have His heart, our desire and response are similar. Mission therefore is not static. It acts.

Upping the stakes

Jesus was a breath of fresh air in Israel to those who were enthralled by all He represented and was accomplishing as they encountered Him. But He was also a threat, particularly to the ruling religious institution, which feared an undermining of the traditions and structures they maintained. Likewise, today, when God is on the move and His Spirit is stirring a new initiative or fresh vision, taking people out of their comfort zone and presenting a challenge to the status quo, there will be those who may feel compromised, resulting in conflict or entrenchment.

People can get very comfortable with a known, even predictable, and safe church culture that is non-threatening and doesn't make many demands. But there was, and still is, an equal danger, when those running with a move of the Spirit of God and raising the bar of expectation want to ditch the baby with the bathwater. 'We're stepping into something new so the old no longer applies!' can be the voice that is raised. Either way, the significance is not how we 'do church', but what underpins our walk with God and the places He wants to take us.

What is it that we hunger and thirst for in relation to His kingdom and His glory being released? Because neither following a tradition nor engaging in new projects or initiatives count for much if our underlying attitude is one of self-promotion, either as a church or as individuals. It is His righteousness that we seek after.

This is very clearly spelt out by Jesus when He emphasises that the Old Testament law is not to be done away with or superseded but is fundamental to discipleship: 'Do not think that I came to destroy the Law or the Prophets. I did not come to destroy but to fulfil' (Matthew 5:17). The new does not replace the old but enhances and re-enforces it, in a far more challenging way, whereby His followers need to rise above the outward working of it and embrace a higher level of righteousness that goes beyond mere religious observance: 'For I say to you, that unless your righteousness exceeds *the righteousness* of the scribes and Pharisees, you will by no means enter the kingdom of heaven' (Matthew 5:20).

We are governed by love and driven by love, in the manner Jesus loved. It is here, when we look upon all that is around us in this world, that something stirs inside our spirits with a yearning to see healing, forgiveness, reconciliation, wholeness, redemption and hope in a broken and despairing world.

These are not simply religious hooks or the jargon of our Christian faith that we throw around in our church vocabulary, but a real and tangible practical outworking of love. People may not recognise or understand some of the language we use, but they recognise and respond to these facets of servanthood, where grace and mercy bring transformation to people's lives.

If His disciples thought they were getting off lightly regarding the law, because of their relationship with Jesus, they were in for a shock. Jesus ups the stakes regarding our attitudes and lifestyle in following Him. His call to love God and love our neighbour sums up the whole law.[79] All this has implications for how we are to love others, for we are challenged to dig deep into our heart's attitudes towards them.

Jesus' criticism of the Pharisees was that they operated from

---

[79] Matthew 22:37-40.

an outward expression of obedience to God that was ritualistic and often cold.[80] As such, any sense of sincere love or compassion that Jesus would have expected from them seemed to be lost. It is a genuine love for one another that should be the driving force of our relational response towards others and the practical outworking of the compassion that is within us. It is here, surely, that our hunger and thirst for righteousness should rise above the norm of the religious spirit. When this becomes our desire and our attitudinal approach towards others, then love truly does become the compass that guides our actions. This becomes the cry of our hearts and what is foremost in our thoughts and responses. It is here that we are filled because it is here that love reigns and flourishes.

Kingdom seekers

> Now after John was put in prison, Jesus came to Galilee, preaching the gospel of the kingdom of God, and saying, 'The time is fulfilled, and the kingdom of God is at hand. Repent, and believe in the gospel.'
> *Mark 1:14-15*

Living in the kingdom of God challenges us in terms of our lifestyle and the integrity with which we exercise our faith and trust in Him.

In the UK we have a monarchy that 'reigns' over us. Our King resides in His official capacity as monarch in Buckingham Palace, and though we may visit as tourists, it is unlikely we will meet him there. Although we live in his kingdom, we do not live in his presence (unless we are privileged to be invited to a rare, special occasion). At best we see him on TV. But suppose he invited you personally to come and stay with him and then said to you, 'Make yourself at home.' Or better still, suppose he said to you, 'We would like to come and stay with you. You may need to make some alterations to accommodate us. Please let us

---

[80] Matthew 23:27-28.

know if that is convenient.' What would be your reaction and response?

This is really what the kingdom of God is about. The kingdom is where the King is. Where is He? Living in those who believe in Him and choose to surrender all to follow Him. He lives in us, not as a distant monarch, but in intimacy, in relationship. Unlike our earthly king, we live in His constant presence. He resides with us. He is our God, and we are His people, as one.

This is where our focus lies. When Jesus says, 'But seek first the kingdom of God and His righteousness, and all these things shall be added to you' (Matthew 6:33), this is where He says the disciples' priorities are to be centred. Jesus is centring on the Father as being at the heart of our attention, devotion and trust; in our giving, our prayer life, our treasures, our vision, our possessions; everything. It all centres on this. We are called to be kingdom seekers.

Jesus reminds us that our heavenly Father has everything in hand. He knows our needs. He makes provision for us. We can trust Him in the knowledge that He works everything for our good when we come to know Him, whatever our experiences of life.[81] Therefore, we are not to become preoccupied with the things this world chases after. It seems to me that the more we have materially, the more anxiety and stress it produces, because we grow to depend on these things, and they become our security.

> Therefore do not worry, saying, 'What shall we eat?' or 'What shall we drink?' or 'What shall we wear?' For all these things the Gentiles seek. For your heavenly Father knows that you need all these things.
> *Matthew 6:31-32*

This is the character of His kingdom. This is what we are to invest in and prioritise if we seek to grow in intimacy with Him,

---

[81] Romans 8:28.

and be filled with wisdom, knowledge and understanding of Him. There is no shortcut. We cannot 'dip into His kingdom' at will when the fancy or need takes us. We cannot sit on the fence of indecision or indifference.

When we invite Him into our lives, we give Him permission to rearrange things in us: everything. He transforms us to be more like Him; to reflect His glory; to be a kingdom-centred people chasing after His heart, His will and His righteousness.

To be materially focused, on the other hand, is to take our eyes off the One who knows and truly provides for our needs. Material possessions become a distraction and cause us to lose trust in God, making our relationship with Him secondary. We create a mentality that says, 'I believe in God and follow Him, but seek out other places for some of my needs to be met.' It's like being employed by one person but going to work for another.

For kingdom seekers, there is only one answer. It's the same answer Jesus gave His disciples after His encounter with the woman at the well, when they urged Him to eat something:

> Jesus said to them, 'My food is to do the will of Him who sent Me, and to finish His work. Do you not say, 'There are still four months and *then* comes the harvest'? Behold, I say to you, lift up your eyes and look at the fields, for they are already white for harvest!'
> *John 4:34-35*

To seek first the kingdom (the King's domain), is to allow Him total reign in all our affairs and to direct our paths according to His will and purpose. The things we hunger for are the things we will wholeheartedly invest in. It is here that our hunger and thirst for righteousness is satisfied. It is here that we are filled because God's name is honoured and glorified. 'And Jesus said to them, "I am the bread of life. He who comes to Me shall never hunger, and he who believes in Me shall never thirst"' (John 6:35).

Mixing with the wrong kind

Who do you hang around with? Think for a moment about the circle of friends you have, and the different people groups you associate with. I expect they are probably people you are comfortable with and with whom you share similar interests or tastes. As Christians we can often limit our connections, family aside, to members of our church fellowship or 'Christian friends' wider afield with whom we have associated for a while.

As human beings we tend to socialise and associate with those we are comfortable with and, by contrast, avoid places and people who make us feel uneasy, awkward or even threatened. And yet these are often the places Jesus wants to take us, because these are the very places and people He associated with and engaged with in conversation. It is here we see the nature of being merciful, treating people with kindness and forgiveness.

What does 'being merciful' look like? In my previous book, *I AM Relational*, I wrote about a café, the Ship Centre, owned by the church in Rainham:

> Over the years, many other cafés had sprung up in the community and we increasingly struggled to make ends meet, pay bills and wages, with fewer and fewer people using the facilities.
> At this point God challenged our thinking and vision for the place. Our perspective had to change from a business mindset to a community one that put people at the centre. We shut the Ship Centre down and spent the next six months prayerfully seeking His way forward, His purpose for its use, and His direction. He did not disappoint ... We were to feed the hungry and gather the lost. No business plan, no programme-driven mandate, no cost to anyone, just gather people in need, feed them and care for them. We reopened the centre with a new

purpose, vision and strategy.[82]

God so often uses our resources to enhance and release His purposes when we allow Him access to guide and direct our path. But in doing so He also invests in those resources, both practically and spiritually. Before anything radical could take place in this new vision for the Ship Centre, there was some internal reordering that needed putting right. Sheryl, underpinned by her successful background in business, was given the reins in spearheading improvements at the Ship Centre.

The biggest challenge was moving the café from a Hygiene Level two to level five, which, after much effort, improvement and financial investment, was achieved. Of course, at that stage, we were still a café serving the community, like every other café. There was, nonetheless, a sense not only of accomplishment, but that we were giving God our best, even though at that point we were struggling to make ends meet, not through anybody's fault and certainly not for lack of trying.

But it was that phrase, 'feed the hungry and gather the lost', that was to change everything; not just in the nature of what we were doing and how we were doing it, but in the people we were reaching out to and embracing. This was a people-centred, not business-centred, vision. It was a place where mercy was implemented by default, through the loving and serving ethos that permeated not just the premises but also the voluntary and paid members of staff who chose to be there out of compassion.

It created an atmosphere where people could come and feel safe. They were neither judged not condemned. They were accepted for who they were. It was only on the very rare occasion, when violence was threatened, that we had to remove individuals, and even then, we would seek their reconciliation so they could return on a more positive basis.

No one was rejected and we had many kinds of people walk through our doors with all kinds of needs and issues. We served

---

[82] Pradella, *I AM Relational*, p95.

them as best we could and loved them. Out of this grew a community of trust and integrity. There was a lot of brokenness that came through those doors, but also a lot of healing and hope generated in those lives. Most, if not all, recognised our caring of them. Broken families, broken marriages, drug and alcohol abuse, those with mental health issues, homeless and unemployed. They all came, and all felt it was their place, because mercy and grace were present, bringing them to a place of belonging.

Jesus sought out such people deliberately: the marginalised, the outcasts, the downtrodden and those put down, as well as people who had been wronged or prejudicially judged because of their condition, status or appearance. Everyone mattered to Him, and everyone still does. It didn't particularly bother Him what consequences He faced, or the accusations made by others as a result. Mercy was more significant than judgement.

When, for example, He called Matthew, a tax collector, to follow Him, Jesus ended up dining in his house. There were many other guests, made up of other 'tax collectors and sinners' (Mark 2:15). Word got out among the scribes and Pharisees, who responded full of contempt at what they saw as totally unbecoming of a rabbi. Predictably, they expressed their displeasure to Jesus' disciples. But Jesus, undaunted, responded in His usual challenging manner:

> When Jesus heard *it*, He said to them, 'Those who are well have no need of a physician, but those who are sick. I did not come to call *the* righteous, but sinners, to repentance.'
> *Mark 2:17*

The attitude of being merciful carries with it a default position of being non-judgemental. Mercy requires us to see others from the perspective that doesn't condemn and, if anything, calls us to draw alongside and identify with them, regardless of whether they deserve it or not. There is equally no room for prejudice here. 'Judge not, that you be not judged. For with what judgment you judge, you will be judged; and with the measure you use, it will be measured back to you' (Matthew 7:1-2).

Judgement has a positive and a negative side. Every day of our lives we make judgement calls. They are natural. 'Is it safe to cross the road now?' 'Should I pay my tax that's due?' 'Do I need to take something for this headache?' and so on. It is a necessary part of life that enables us to survive and be safe. That is positive. But there is a negative side to judgement which carries with it a critical and negative spirit. It applies to how we view and treat others disapprovingly, and this is what Jesus is addressing here. We are not in a place to justifiably sit on the judgement seat. That is to place ourselves on a level equal to God in both authority and wisdom. We are certainly not and never will be. Only God is the One before whom we all stand in judgement.[83] Our accountability is to Him alone. On the other hand, God, who is merciful, calls us to be merciful.

When we show mercy to others, we are stretching our hand out to them, accepting who they are but also seeking to extend the same compassion with which Jesus shares His love and forgiveness. In so doing, we confirm that we too shall obtain mercy, placing ourselves on an equal footing with all whom God would reconcile to Himself, regardless of their condition or lifestyle.

This is the blessing of being merciful. It enables others to experience the love of God through our compassionate walk with them, aiding them to respond accordingly. By withholding mercy, are we not depriving them of such an opportunity as we once had, to discover for themselves the love of Jesus that is on offer to all?

The speck hunter

It is not just what we display outwardly, but also what goes on inside our hearts that reveals our true nature and exposes the

---

[83] Romans 14:10; John 5:22; 2 Timothy 4:1.

sincerity of our attitudes. It is often here that the battle over our identity can take place, between the old self and the 'new creation' in Christ (2 Corinthians 5:17).

Arrogance, pride, self-centredness and the like are very subtle in how they manifest themselves in the value we place on others. It is here that these negative attributes can create a 'looking down on' approach that is designed to elevate us in our self-perception of who we think we are.

The words of the prophet Micah embrace what our attitude should be: '

> He has shown you, O man, what *is* good;
> And what does the LORD require of you
> But to do justly,
> To love mercy,
> And to walk humbly with your God?
> *Micah 6:8*

Justice, mercy and humility are the safeguards that prevent us from being judgemental because they are contrary to the spirit of pride, criticism and finger-pointing that 'speck hunting' feeds on.

When we adopt a judgemental mindset towards others, we inevitably create an atmosphere of nit-picking, finding fault and dissatisfaction. It kills encouragement and breeds discontent, resulting in broken relationships, mistrust and disunity.

We often don't see the faults in ourselves, or choose to ignore them. But they are much more obvious to others. Jesus uses two images to talk about this issue.

> And why do you look at the speck in your brother's eye, but do not consider the plank in your own eye? Or how can you say to your brother, 'Let me remove the speck from your eye'; and look, a plank *is* in your own eye?
> *Matthew 7:3-4*

A plank is much more visible than a speck. But the plank, not the speck, is how Jesus describes what is in the judgemental person's eye. No one likes to be judged or criticised, but we don't take that into account when pointing the finger at others. We expose our own weaknesses and failings when we highlight those of others, and often embarrass ourselves in the process. The other person's 'speck' may not be obvious to others until we highlight it and, in doing so, expose their frailty in a judgemental way.

Jesus is encouraging us to first reflect upon our own lives, our faults and weaknesses as well as our strengths and giftings. He does so without mincing His words because these things are too serious to treat lightly or indifferently: 'Hypocrite! First remove the plank from your own eye, and then you will see clearly to remove the speck from your brother's eye' (Matthew 7:5).

This is a reality check, so that we may be real in who we are and what we are called to become. It is a reminder that God's grace and mercy have been poured out on each one of us, and each one of us has been bought at an immeasurable price. We are in no position therefore to 'judge another's servant' (Romans 14:4), but ought rather to soberly walk in grateful thanks for the new life He has given us… and given our brothers and sisters in Christ. If that should be so within the body of Christ, it must surely also embrace our approach to all people in the mercy we show them, regardless of their faith or background. Our attitudes towards others affect our perspective, but also influences their perspective.

The world can often take a contemptuous view of the follower of Jesus who in all outward appearance displays the same worldly and self-centred attitude and behaviour as the world portrays, while claiming to be set apart from it. It cheapens our witness and corrupts the world's understanding of God's holiness and love. This in turn justifies the world responding with the accusing question, 'What makes you different? You act the same as everyone else but, worse, you're just a hypocrite and a bigot!' These are the responses of unreceptive people whose hearts become or continue to be hardened to the light of the gospel, whereby we have merely fuelled their arguments of hostility towards Christ.

Not only is our reputation tarnished here, but, more importantly, God's name is trampled on and dishonoured as a result. I believe Jesus points out that it comes back upon us in our effectiveness as followers, and He Himself calls such actions hypocritical. When we are compassionately merciful towards others, the world will sit up and take notice.

Thought break

- How hungry are you for God and His purposes for you? How is that hunger expressed? Conversely, are you satisfied with your 'lot'?

- What is the difference between legalism and accountability? What do you understand the word 'law' to mean? How relevant today is the law that God gave us? Where does our righteousness as Christians fit into that?

- How far are you prepared to reach out to people who are very different from you in lifestyle, and have diverse needs? Who are the people groups/individuals Jesus is calling you to follow Him to, to engage with and build relationships with?

14

The Lamp of Purity and Peace

The pure in heart, the peacemakers

There is a paint company that once advertised its product as doing exactly what it says on the tin. What is written on 'your tin'? Is the person others see you as on the outside the same as the person who is on the inside? Do you reflect the person God created you to be?

When Jesus talked about the 'pure in heart' as being able to 'see God' (Matthew 5:8), who might He have been referring to? The pure in heart, I would suggest, are those who love God in a manner of sincerity and with a passionate, undivided submission; whose inward nature reflects God's own heart. We cannot live in close relationship with God and not reflect His purity to some degree.

Why is living with a pure heart so significant? Primarily, if the God of purity indwells you and me, then the purity of God must transform our own hearts to reflect His. Purity is not merely what goes on in our thoughts or minds, but what goes on in our hearts. It is in the core of our being that we see reflected what we truly are, because what is in us is what is then released outwardly. Or is it?

Jesus has much to say about what goes on inside us and not

just what is seen on the surface by others. We can all wear masks and hide behind them. Our attitudes and thoughts can appear as genuine and sincere, and yet we can inwardly live a whole different existence.

When Sheryl and I first met, there were no mobile phones. We were then living too far apart to meet up every day, and often Sheryl would be abroad with her work, which took her all over the world on business trips. We relied on landlines to keep in touch. We would often jokingly say things like, 'Wouldn't it be great if there was a phone where you could see the person you are talking to?' Little did we know that we would be living in a world where smartphones not only make that a reality – and we now take such technology for granted as the norm – but our devices can do so much more than just make calls.

But what if such devices then advanced to be able to capture and project our innermost thoughts and feelings? What if those inner secret places we hide from others were then circulated across social media sites, visible for all to see? I imagine for most, if not all, of us, panic would set in and reactions ranging from awkward embarrassment to outright terror would consume us. It takes 'selfies' to a whole new level. We assume that those places are unreachable and hidden from view, and so we are content to harbour our inner thoughts in the false presumption that no one else sees. Yet God sees right through all our inner concealment, right into the very core of our beings, right into our hearts.

We can literally conceal nothing from Him, even though we delude ourselves in thinking otherwise, or somehow convince ourselves that if He does see and does know, it doesn't really matter. But it should. It is here that Jesus touches on those very areas we think are safely hidden within us.

I suspect many of us would say we do not murder or commit adultery, or openly malign others, or make false oaths. As such we probably feel secure in our perception of ourselves. Many people mistakenly think they are good because they do not do bad things that are visible to others. But Jesus exposes such thoughts as mistaken, and a dangerous assumption to make.

We probably would not even begin to entertain the thought of taking someone's life with calculated intent (murder). But we can sometimes harbour thoughts of anger, repulsion, loathing and even hatred towards others, and often in judgemental ways. We may feel we have good reason to do so, but I'm not sure that is always the case – even calling them fools or idiots. We may convince ourselves that such thoughts are justifiable, but are they? Thinking others are beneath us, with an attitude of contempt concerning their character; going further and wishing them harm or misfortune. Jesus condemns these thoughts as equal to murder. Ouch!

> You have heard that it was said to those of old, 'You shall not murder, and whoever murders will be in danger of the judgment.' But I say to you that whoever is angry with his brother without a cause shall be in danger of the judgment. And whoever says to his brother, 'Raca!' shall be in danger of the council. But whoever says, 'You fool!' shall be in danger of hell fire.
> *Matthew 5:21-22*

Anything that maligns or belittles someone else, including idle gossip and judgemental comments, jeopardises our relationship with God, as well as those we 'murder'.[84] We cannot assume to come before God with such attitudes inside and expect our worship to be acceptable to Him. It will not be. It will go no further than the ceiling and will then bounce back. And there are other equally negative thoughts that can preoccupy us in unhealthy ways. The area of adultery is one. If we are married, we may well not contemplate being promiscuous and having affairs outside our relationship with our spouse. We think we are safe from adulterous ways. But to even look at another person with lust for them in our hearts condemns us as adulterers:

---

[84] 1 John 2:9-11; 4:20-21.

> You have heard that it was said to those of old, 'You shall not commit adultery.' But I say to you that whoever looks at a woman to lust for her has already committed adultery with her in his heart.
> *Matthew 5:27-28*

Physically admiring someone for their looks or manner is not wrong in itself; it is quite normal to see someone as physically attractive or good-natured. But it's when we turn that into an obsession where lustful thoughts can creep in and turn something innocent into something sinister that the problem emerges.

Lust, in whatever form it takes, whether outside marriage, infidelity, impure thoughts through or leading to enticements such as pornography, or any other form of debased sexual desires, corrupts us and deforms who we are in our identity in Christ, creating shame, guilt and ultimately separation from God. We are not only part of His body, but as living temples, we are also the place where His Spirit dwells.[85] I would suggest there is not only a conflict of interest here but also a falsehood that cannot be condoned on any level as compatible with our walk of discipleship. We deceive ourselves if we think otherwise.

Living in the truth

Purity involves sincerity and integrity, which in turn are to do with truthfulness. Following the One who is truth raises the bar of expectation. Pilate once asked Jesus, 'What is truth?' (John 18:38). That is an interesting question in a world where there appear to be multiple truths that can be defined, each as plausible as the next in a secular context. But reality and what we convey from within are two different things. What lies inside is the real yardstick of where and how truth is defined; or perhaps where untruth dwells and deceives.

We hear phrases like, 'I swear to God, I didn't do it,' or,

---

[85] 1 Corinthians 3:16.

'Honest to God, I will be there,' or, 'On my mother's life, I'm not lying,' and so on. It seems to me that the need for such phrases is almost an admission of the opposite. Why go to such extremes to convince someone you are speaking honestly, unless of course you are evading the truthful answer.

Let's face it, we are all prone to lying, falsifying, distorting or fabricating accounts and events. Without the nature of deceit in our lives, oaths would serve no purpose. Our yes would be yes, and our no would be no. It points therefore to the fact that a person's word alone can be unreliable and, as such, an admission of failure in truthfulness.

Truth is the realm in which healthy relationships are nurtured and developed. There cannot be unity where there is falsehood. Nor can we live in wholeness and blessing if in our hearts there is a tendency to allow deception to pollute our spirit, which then, by its nature, spreads to others.

To walk in righteousness with God means we have nothing to hide or fear, because we walk with sincerity and integrity. It is a lifestyle as well as an attitude of heart. Coming into truthfulness is only possible where sin has been uncovered and dealt with, and through forgiveness we become whole and renewed. This is the light of the hope we have in Christ. It becomes our nature to live in that light and embrace the purity of God that is reflected by it. People who still live in 'darkness' do not like this kind of truth and resist it, because through it they are confronted with the reality of who they are and, as such, remain in a place of condemnation.[86]

The stresses and strains of an ever-faster pace of life can press us into becoming conformed to what is going on around us and we can get sucked into the wider path, which becomes so easy to slip into and walk in. 'Everybody does it, so it must be alright,' is the assumption people make and the mistake they often fall into. Jesus, on the other hand, calls us to choose to walk the narrow path,[87] the path of righteousness, of truth and

---

[86] John 3:19-21.
[87] Matthew 7:13-14.

of purity of heart. It's harder to find and difficult to stay on, because it is contrary to a worldly human spirit. It goes against the flow. It's like trying to walk into a packed crowd that are going the opposite way to you, or like trying to walk up an escalator that is travelling downward.

There are things along this path that we would not necessarily choose for our lives, nor can we sustain its journey by ourselves. I'm sure many have tried and failed. In our own strength it becomes a path that is religious but devoid of the power to transform us. Paul reminds us of that: 'For they being ignorant of God's righteousness, and seeking to establish their own righteousness, have not submitted to the righteousness of God' (Romans 10:3).

The light of true sight

Jesus tells us that the 'pure in heart' are those who are blessed and who will 'see God' (Matthew 5:8). Sight is not just physical but includes perception as well. What we see and what we perceive are not necessarily the same. We can be deceived in all manner of ways where illusion and reality blur and come into a confused focus of our understanding or perception.

Numerous people are convinced they are right in many areas of life, whether in political persuasion, religious interpretation and experience, subjective beliefs on all manner of things and in the choices they make. In a way, that is our prerogative and the nature of being human. We make judgement calls every day based on the information, perception or experience we have available to us at the time. Sometimes those choices or decisions can be clouded or misleading, however well intentioned.

I wonder if the ability to see God in the way Jesus speaks of, regarding those who are pure-hearted, is primarily founded on the clarity of our own hearts, whereby there is nothing false that misshapes our perception, because we are governed by the wisdom of His Spirit living in us and guided in a truer perspective of the reality around us.

It is in the light that we see things more clearly; our eyes can focus with greater clarity and sharpness. If that is so, then it explains Jesus' own words when He says:

> The lamp of the body is the eye. If therefore your eye is good, your whole body will be full of light. But if your eye is bad, your whole body will be full of darkness. If therefore the light that is in you is darkness, how great *is* that darkness!
> *Matthew 6:22-23*

This is not about optical defects and the need for glasses. This is about the choice of serving God or self. The litmus test, I believe, is in what makes our heart race, what impassions us and makes us want to leap up and punch the air with joy. The good eye will be encouraged and excited about seeing a person we prayed for receive healing, a person we witnessed to come to Christ, providing for someone's needs at a time of crisis and seeing their lives transformed as a result. In other words, seeing God's kingdom having an impact on our lives; growing in wisdom, knowledge and understanding; seeing a next generation sold out for God and serving Him in a dynamic way.

The bad eye is the opposite. Whether individually or as a body, when our motives, agendas or priorities are self-seeking or materially driven, we will never realise the potential God has for us and will settle for less than He wants to release to and through us by His Spirit. We will always rely on our own efforts, ideas and objectives. There is no divine fruit in such a pursuit, and we will never be satisfied nor prosper because His light in us is extinguished. Where there is no or little light, there is darkness. But, as Jesus points out, it is a great darkness because we are not aware that we are in the dark and so live in a false sense of security, a spirit of religion rather than relationship. The bad eye will be more impressed with the maintenance of a church building than the mission of the church in seeking the lost, with how much we can save rather than what we can give away to bless others, with material well-being and personal comfort rather than the welfare of others.

The contagion of transforming peace

What is a peacemaker? And what, if anything, is the difference between peacemaking and peacekeeping? Jesus said, 'Peace I leave with you, My peace I give to you; not as the world gives do I give to you. Let not your heart be troubled, neither let it be afraid' (John 14:27).

Everywhere He went, Jesus exuded a different kind of peace from that defined by the world. It is a peace that speaks of wholeness and well-being, free from a troubled spirit and fearful disposition. It is not affected or influenced by external circumstances or situations, but has the power to influence and change the environment around it.

It is this peace that Jesus gives to His disciples, to you and to me when we embrace His presence in us. It is an inner peace that nothing can compete with when it comes to our well-being, because it is anchored not in a concept or frame of mind, but in a person. Jesus is the Prince of Peace.

The peacemakers are those who walk in His peace. 'These things I have spoken to you, that in Me you may have peace. In the world you will have tribulation; but be of good cheer, I have overcome the world' (John 16:33). His peace is designed to overcome our anxieties and fears.

We carry His peace and release it wherever we go. Peacemaking, therefore, has a purpose. I once illustrated this during a talk I was giving on the subject, by inviting several volunteers to visually demonstrate the concept I was trying to get across. I gave each of them a balloon and asked them to blow it up, which they obligingly did. But I then told them to keep blowing into the balloon and not stop. The size of the balloons continued to enlarge, as did the tension around, and particularly from each participant. There were squeamish expressions on people's faces as they waited for the first pop, and when it came, everyone jumped. To the relief of the other participants, I got them to stop blowing and then to let go of their balloons, which flew around in circles as the air was expelled.

When we are not at peace, either with ourselves or with the circumstances we find ourselves in, all kinds of tensions build up, with anxieties, fears, worries and the like filling us with unease and unbalancing our equilibrium. We can be in such a state for prolonged periods of time, and the damage to our health increases because emotional pressures soon lead to physical symptoms: high blood pressure, panic attacks, various mental health issues and many other conditions. External pressures from work, relational issues, economic worries or health problems can all contribute to our lack of peace. Like in the balloon, the pressures build up until they become critical and burst out, or until we let go.

I believe Jesus alone gives us the ability to let go, when we allow God's presence and the peace He instils to change our perspective. Jesus said, 'Therefore I say to you, do not worry about your life, what you will eat or what you will drink; nor about your body, what you will put on. Is not life more than food and the body more than clothing?' (Matthew 6:25).

Our earthly lives bring daily challenges and pressures in the most practical everyday ways, let alone in the expectations we place on ourselves of having to do this, or accomplish that, or meet this or that deadline. We are all familiar with these experiences and know the burdens they produce. Some cope better than others in such circumstances, some even thrive to a degree, but none of us is exempt from them.

But peacemaking is not simply about our own well-being and settled mind, or our ability to cope and deal with things. The fact that we carry His peace when we are in right relationship with Jesus should be a given. The peacemaker, therefore, is the disciple whose inner peace is released to others, whereby their presence influences those around them. They are the environment-changers.

Our purpose as peacemakers is to willingly seek not only to

resolve conflicts we find, but also to bring into them a different perspective that channels God's loving presence into those very situations or circumstances and change them. 'But whatever house you enter, first say, "Peace to this house." And if a son of peace is there, your peace will rest on it; if not, it will return to you' (Luke 10:5-6). I call this finding people of peace, as I mentioned earlier. There will be those who warm to your involvement with them and seek to serve you in the process, because they have been blessed by what you have released to them or ministered in, bringing relief or hope to their situation, as well as encouragement and support. There will be others who choose to reject what you offer. Either way, your own inner peace is not diminished.

The peace Jesus carried was likewise both accepted and rejected by different people. But ultimately, it was on the cross that peace with God was made, and by His blood the peace of reconciliation always triumphs over the power of sin that seeks to subdue it.

Peace is what emanates from a transformed heart that has been reconciled through forgiveness and filled with the renewing power of the Holy Spirit indwelling us. That is why Jesus calls peacemakers 'sons of God' (Matthew 5:9). They carry the hallmarks and outworking of His presence. They have an impact upon the communities they serve.

For His eyes only

We have been given an extraordinary ministry and privilege as His followers, to share and demonstrate His love to others and see lives transformed and set free. Our focus, our intention and our reason for being is to make Jesus visible, to always point to Him through our words, actions and attitude in witness. It is not and should never be self-seeking or self-promoting.

God will not share His glory with anyone. He alone is Lord. He alone reigns. This was very much Jesus' own approach and attitude. His thoughts and actions were always directed towards serving others, but always so His Father got the glory.[88] Everything He did and said came from a place of intimacy. He brought genuine relationship to us from the place of relationship in heaven. It is this heavenly community that we are called to reflect here on earth. We are here to give Him pleasure and delight. Regarding our relationship with our heavenly Father, Jesus gives us a stark warning about blowing our own trumpet, aligning it to being a hypocrite – someone who wears a mask and is false. They 'have their reward', and it is shallow (Matthew 6:2). When we do things 'in secret', there is no pretence and our hearts are sincere, for only God sees and rewards us accordingly (Matthew 6:3-4).

Our charity, in whatever form it takes, is a response to the compassion genuinely expressed in our concern for others. This is because it reflects God's own heart of love and the compassion Jesus expressed in reaching out to those in need. It is not a guilt trip reaction, or being swept up by the euphoria of the popular, jumping on a media-driven hype that disappears as quickly as it comes, even when the needs remain. As disciples we respond to the things that God touches our hearts with, things that bring conviction and compassion to respond to that which is on His heart. In the same way, we read in Exodus 3:7 that God's heart went out for His enslaved people in Egypt; He conveyed that to Moses, whom He then sent to address that for which He had called him. We don't need to look far to recognise those who are lost and desperate for His love to be expressed through us.

---

[88] 1 Corinthians 1:29; Isaiah 42:8; John 17:4-5.

Thought break

- Are there people you need to be reconciled with, who may have been hurt, damaged or disgraced by your actions, words or thoughts towards them; perhaps with whom there is now a barrier or resentment? Where could you begin to put things right?

- Can being untruthful or deceitful ever be justified? What does lying do to a person who finds it necessary to 'hide' behind untruth?

- What does peace mean for you? How easily do you lose your peace in the face of circumstances around you that might be deemed stressful or confrontational? What restores your peace?

15

Conflicts and Challenges

Those who are persecuted for righteousness' sake

To be right in our relationship with God is often to be in enmity with a world whose values are opposed to His truth. To come to terms with that, we must first acknowledge that our lives are bound together in Him and in one another, and it is as His community that God has created us to live and prosper.

What we feed ourselves on affects who we are and who we become. It shapes not only our outlook on life, but also our identity. Independence feeds on self, whereas interdependence makes us co-reliant on one another and generates an environment of caring and sharing. That is the concept of living in His kingdom. But in a fallen world, the ideals of such living can create conflict and tension where they are not universally acknowledged or where the values of kingdom living clash with an opposing world view. It is here that persecution and hostility arise. When Jesus spoke about those 'persecuted for righteousness' sake' as being blessed (Matthew 5:10), it almost sounds like a contradiction in terms, a paradox. How can you be persecuted, reviled, rejected and misunderstood and remain blessed? It is because the disciple is one whose focus and whole direction of life is centred on God's will and purpose for them.

It concerns seeking His kingdom and His righteousness to be made evident. It is here that our principal motivation lies. It is here that even our own personal welfare and well-being takes second place.

As such, it is also here that conflict lies. Let's face it, nobody, given the choice, desires to be disliked, let alone rejected or maligned and ridiculed. Part of being relational is the need to be accepted and to belong, to want to fit in. But there is more at stake here than just being popular or part of the crowd.

When we choose to follow Jesus, we put self to death and decide to live for Him. That means we have chosen to go against the grain of the world. But more than that, we are called not to remain hidden, but to shine in the darkness; to affect and influence and change the ways of worldly values. There is a cost when we step onto the path that He places us on, in terms of not just personal sacrifice, but also rejection. Jesus made clear in Matthew 10:24-25 that if they persecuted Him (and they did) they will persecute us (and they do).

When we advance the kingdom of God through what we proclaim, what we witness to and what we minister in, it is an offence to the 'earthly' values of those who would stand opposed to the uniqueness and divinity of Jesus. It is a truth the world does not want to hear, nor acknowledge or tolerate, let alone accept. And so, persecution is the inevitable outcome.

I believe there are two forms of persecution. One is the more obvious kind, where not only rejection but also hostile opposition outlaws and prohibits any open proclamation or practice of faith in Jesus, even to the extent of imprisonment and death for those who choose to stand firm in their commitment to Him.

We see such persecution and intolerance of Christians in various regions and countries in the world. Even so, in such a hostile environment, the Church continues to grow and its message spreads regardless. The greater the persecution, it seems, the greater the determination, steadfastness and growth, even in the face of martyrdom.

The second kind of 'persecution' is much more subtle and detrimental and, I would suggest, is more prevalent in affluent Western democracies. Where the Church in persecuted areas thrives and grows, here in a secular democratic environment, it is prone to decline; decline that takes the nature of apathy, indifference and complacency. It acts like an inner cancer rather than an external threat. It thrives on diluting the passion of our faith, polluting it with worldly 'acceptable' tolerance and corrupting its values with inner squabbles and schisms that are anything but kingdom-centred. I wonder if such is the mindset, compromised by worldly values, that erodes the Church's foundation, rendering it powerless and voiceless, drowned out by the cares of the world and sucked into a consumerist religious existence that is far from the influential powerhouse Jesus called it to be.

It is a form of persecution through intimidation that feeds on and fosters sitting on a spiritual fence, with one foot in each camp. It lacks the ability to transform lives because it has nothing radical or uniquely life-changing to offer those who are lost and seeking. Maintenance of an institution takes precedence over mission to the lost.

Materialism and wealth play a large part in enticement away from kingdom values and commitment, lulling many into a comfort-zone approach to life, while seeking diversions that enhance a comfortable and undemanding existence, free from any real threats. It is here perhaps that private faith is encouraged. Believe what you like, as long as it does not affect others: this then becomes the acceptable norm.

This is an issue of relationship that questions where our dependency lies:

> No one can serve two masters; for either he will hate the one and love the other, or else he will be loyal to the one and despise the other. You cannot serve God and mammon.
> *Matthew 6:24*

The cross that walks the path

If following Jesus means embracing suffering, hardship and even rejection, our hesitation or reluctance to walk such a path is an understandable reaction, because we want our journey of faith in Jesus to be marked with blessing, fruitfulness and joy, with all the expectations of following a victorious Messiah who has conquered all Himself.

We do not always like to accept the fact that to follow Jesus means being prepared to carry our cross, even though He spelt out clearly that it would lead us on just such a path. This is what it meant for Him, and we must be prepared for the same. He was reviled, ridiculed, humiliated, abandoned, mocked and completely isolated as He hung on that cross for you and me; out of choice because of His love for us. This was no hero's death. There were no medals of honour or cheering crowds. Jeering, yes, and hostility too. The road to Calvary is a lonely and unwelcoming walk.

Paul reminds us that our walk with Christ is not a cosy or comfortable journey. We are called to be carriers of His death and resurrection:

> *We are* hard-pressed on every side, yet not crushed; *we are* perplexed, but not in despair; persecuted, but not forsaken; struck down, but not destroyed — always carrying about in the body the dying of the Lord Jesus, that the life of Jesus also may be manifested in our body. For we who live are always delivered to death for Jesus' sake, that the life of Jesus also may be manifested in our mortal flesh. So then death is working in us, but life in you.
> *2 Corinthians 4:8-12*

It is only in living from the place of the empty tomb, in the power of His resurrection, that we can carry His love to others with the capacity to influence and transform the lives of those for whom we have compassion. That is the nature and requirement of love, because it is founded in God's love; a sacrificial and passionate love for this lost and rebellious world into which He sent His Son, to redeem it and reconcile us to Himself.

When we lose sight of this, we are in danger of reducing our discipleship into a weekly emotional 'fix', with little or no demands, while neglecting to instil any sense of urgency in the mission we are called to. Francis Chan reminds us:

> Jesus loved so deeply that He was willing to suffer a lifetime of rejection, even rejection from His Father on the cross. Jesus never lost sight of God's holiness and the offensiveness of sin. He suffered for speaking truth, showing us that true love is often rejected. This was the way of Jesus. This is the way of love.[89]

Walking the path with a desire to follow Him requires a clear understanding of the implications involved. The reality of daily taking up our cross is challenging but also necessary if we are to lose our self-centred life for His sake and find it fully new in Him.[90] It is here that we are truly empowered and grow in the maturity into which we are transformed and released.

Failing that, we become anesthetised with an 'oh well, that's life' approach; disappointed, unfulfilled and locked in an inevitable cycle that does not change our condition but merely accepts it and excuses it. Worse still, in such a context, we create a theology around failure, reducing our expectancy in the power and presence of God to act with effectiveness and fruitfulness. We then suffocate the divine hope we inherit, reducing it to something far less that it was given for.

The pleasures, comforts and pulls of this world are extremely attractive and inviting. The world is extremely good at selling itself in an intoxicating way. It has a strong influential hold on

---

[89] Francis Chan, *Letters to the Church* (Colorado Springs, CO: David C Cook, 2018), p137.
[90] Matthew 16:24-25.

us, and the willingness to let go and put those dependencies to death, together with the mindset they invoke, is not easy, to say the least.

'Safe' discipleship cannot accept such a sacrificial route to following and, as such, defaults to by-standing while avoiding intimidation, threat and hardship. Francis Chan writes:

> There are millions of men and women who have been taught that they can become Christians and it will cost them nothing. And they believe it! There are even some who have the audacity to teach that life will get better once people pray a prayer and ask Jesus into their hearts. Jesus taught the exact opposite![91]

Sacrificial discipleship may be something none of us is comfortable with, but when Jesus made clear that 'a servant is not greater than his master' (John 15:20), the implications are obvious. Whatever He faced, we may be called to face as well.

Perhaps the first battle is not necessarily external persecution, but the internal surrender of self to the will of God. When I choose to walk this path, a change in my focus is precipitated by a shift from a self-conscious to a Christ-conscious identity. It is not that I no longer matter when I surrender my life to Him, but rather, my life takes on a whole new meaning. I have a renewed compassion for others and a desire for Jesus to become more visible, in all His fullness, in me and through me.

Paul writes:

> I have been crucified with Christ; it is no longer I who live, but Christ lives in me; and the *life* which I now live in the flesh I live by faith in the Son of God, who loved me and gave Himself for me.
> *Galatians 2:20*

---

[91] Chan, *Letters to the Church*, p128.

Such a change is a process, not a one-off event or decision. Dying to self is a daily occurrence, a refining act that draws us ever closer to the One who is our first love.

Refined by endurance

We are called into the family of God as heirs and 'joint heirs with Christ' (Romans 8:15-17). We are not orphans in the world any more, nor are we powerless to act. We are rooted in knowing our identity and purpose. It lies in who we are in Christ as followers of the One who gave life and is life. But there is a cost involved.

> Therefore we also, since we are surrounded by so great a cloud of witnesses, let us lay aside every weight, and the sin which so easily ensnares *us*, and let us run with endurance the race that is set before us, looking unto Jesus, the author and finisher of *our* faith, who for the joy that was set before Him endured the cross, despising the shame, and has sat down at the right hand of the throne of God.
> *Hebrews 12:1-2*

The author of Hebrews reminds us that we are to keep our eyes fixed on Jesus, running the race with staying power. As Jesus Himself encountered, the enemy is ever present, trying to tempt us away from knowing and embracing our inheritance here and now.

Do you know who you are in Christ and how to stand in it? What motivated Jesus to keep going and keep focused? He saw what lay beyond His hardship and suffering: joy. Joy is not an emotional feeling of happiness or elation. It is a reward. It is what every believer in Jesus has as an inheritance.

It is best summed up as the presence of God that is eternal and unshakable; that is all-consuming love, eradicating every darkness, every wrong, every pain and sorrow; the end of everything that separates us from Him or spoils our lives. That is our focus because that was Jesus' focus. His eyes were fixed on the joy that would result from the suffering He would go through. He would not cower before the threats and intimidation, the hostility and rejection, the physical and emotional pain He would undergo in the horrific ordeal that awaited Him, because what awaited Him beyond that was far, far greater.

The call of discipleship is centred always on the One we are following and never on ourselves. It is a road that is marked with a necessity for endurance; a journey pitted with snares, distractions and diversions; a road on which we can easily stumble or become lost.

That is why our gaze and focus is continually on Jesus, because as 'author and finisher of *our* faith', He is the One who has called us (author) and will enable us to complete our assignment (finisher). The perseverance and commitment that He calls us to is one He Himself has gone through, even to the point of death.

Jesus not only challenges our own personal walk with Him, but He also calls us to weigh up our relationship with Him alongside our relationship with others, those whom we love dearly and are closest to. That is easier said than done in the reality of those we share our lives with, and therefore the cost implications of our discipleship need to be understood from the outset.

Sometimes persecution or rejection can be closer to home, even within our families and close friends. Hostility towards the gospel has no single frontier or prescribed form. Persecution, rejection and opposition go with the territory and are worldly in their premise.

Jesus does not beat about the bush, and we need to be careful not to undermine the implications. 'If anyone comes to Me and does not hate his father and mother, wife and children, brothers and sisters, yes, and his own life also, he cannot be My disciple' (Luke 14:26). He must come first if we are to take Him seriously. Everything in our lives, every other relationship we are part of, and our very lives themselves, must come under His sovereign reign over us.

Why does Jesus emphasise families here? Probably because for most of us, our family is the most important and precious thing to us. It is the last thing we would want to sacrifice. Yet it can be the very thing that could hold us back from fully following Him.

Our earthly relationships, therefore, of necessity need to be subordinate to our loyalty and commitment to Jesus. Anything that jeopardises that will undermine the effectiveness with which His kingdom can be released through us. It becomes a stumbling block that we will continually trip over. This can be particularly stressful and difficult for those whose spouses or children do not follow Christ, or are even hostile towards the commitment of their faithful partners. It compromises and stifles the fullness of a desired engagement from the person who is torn between the two and often ends up pleasing neither.

If our allegiance to Christ conflicts with the desires or demands of those we love, which way do we jump? Does true discipleship leave room for any kind of compromise? It is a challenging question that many couples wrestle with and struggle to work through. Perhaps for some, it is here that their primary mission field is the focus of their witness.

We can often settle for complicity with the world to avoid conflict, but in so doing, whether consciously or subconsciously, we can at times create a watered-down theology that says God doesn't mind, because He loves us anyway. We then weaken the effectiveness of the gospel, making it impotent in its ability to change lives, both ours and those of others. We turn following Him into an accessory and not a necessity when we remain unprepared to surrender all and suffer all for His sake.

Rock solid

To redress such a grave detraction from the deep-rooted

relationship Jesus calls us to means we need to re-evaluate what our commitment to Him fully entails. What are the foundations that our faith stands on, and how can we be sure of our firm-footedness in walking where He walks amid the chaos of a world that is tottering and unstable, while denying the existence or relevance of God?

We at times base our relationship with Jesus upon how well we know Him. The real question, though, is not, 'Do you know Jesus?' but, 'Does He know you?' This is probably the most revealing and challenging question we can and should ask ourselves in reflecting upon our own lives and walk with Him: 'Not everyone who says to Me, "Lord, Lord," shall enter the kingdom of heaven, but he who does the will of My Father in heaven' (Matthew 7:21).

So far, so good. But when many try to justify fulfilling that requirement by citing acts of commitment through prophecy, casting out demons and performing many wonders in His name, they and, I suppose, we are alarmed by Jesus' response: 'And then I will declare to them, "I never knew you; depart from Me, you who practice lawlessness!"' (Matthew 7:23). That is a scary prospect and daunting in its starkness.

The first thing, then, is to understand what Jesus is highlighting here. Suppose I asked you how well you know the former Prince of Wales, now King Charles III? You may be able to tell me some facts about him, you may have visited one of the stately homes as a tourist or, if you were an avid royalist and followed the monarchy enthusiastically, you may be able to tell me a lot more details about his life. Many of us can have that level of understanding of Jesus. We are taught about Him, pray to Him, worship Him in our churches and are familiar with who He is and what He has accomplished. Some may consider their commitment in following Him deep, and others less so. But, to return to our analogy, suppose I decided to go to Buckingham Palace and managed, for argument's sake, to get to the front door. On knocking, the official opens the door and I say to them, 'Can you tell His Royal Highness that Henry is here and maybe we could have lunch together and a chat, as I have some time to spare.' The door is shut and there is a pause. The official returns and says to me, 'I'm sorry, sir, but His Royal Highness has no knowledge of who you are,' and firmly shuts the door in my face, threatening to call security if I do not leave. This, I think, is the frightening reality of what Jesus is alluding to. Not, 'Do you know me?' but, 'Do I know you?'

Jesus here cites two misconceptions about our discipleship, both of which can lead us into a false sense of security or misunderstanding, with disastrous consequences. Let's look at each in turn.

First, Jesus said, 'Not everyone who says to Me, "Lord, Lord..."' What we say or confess with our mouths doesn't necessarily reflect what is in our hearts. Nor, for that matter, does it have to engage our hearts. I can say anything I want without it touching me or others.

The religious spirit is very good at liturgical response, at ritual and rhythm. I am not putting down patterns of worship or prayer, nor do I believe Jesus is. But overfamiliarity can lead us to reciting words without giving significance to how they affect our relationship with God. That weekly diet of outward repetition means we don't have to think or engage in an intimate encounter with Him. It does not in itself lead us into His presence, necessarily, because there is no need for the Holy Spirit in a 'programme-driven' rather than 'Spirit-led' meeting.

Moreover, people can think that if they 'go to church' and take part in a 'religious' act of worship, then they are justified before God as 'knowing Him' and He them. Nothing could be further from the truth. To enter the kingdom of heaven (that is, to come under His reign and presence), we must do the will of the Father.

What is that will?

- It is to believe in Jesus.[92] To see the Son and believe in Him

---

[92] John 6:40.

means to encounter Him. Jesus said, 'You did not choose Me, but I chose you' (John 15:16). That means engaging in a relationship with Him and surrendering our lives in pursuit of intimacy with Him, a relationship that by its nature is two-way. It involves growing in maturity and depth through prayerful and scriptural engagement and discourse, encountering His presence and increasing in knowledge and understanding through the outworking of His Spirit in us. It is a relationship we are enveloped in, rather than one we randomly dip into.

- It means recognising a total dependency on God for every area of our lives, not just the church fellowship part. Our lives are not compartmentalised, with faith in Jesus just being one aspect. Jesus Himself modelled surrender and dependency on His Father.[93]

- Such a relationship is only possible by His indwelling Spirit living in us. We cannot have a relationship with Him, without Him. In essence, the will of the Father is to fully invest ourselves in His Son and to be 'transformed by the renewing of [our minds]' (Romans 12:2) in conformity to His will, not the world's.

The second misunderstanding we can be led into lies in the same response many made to His opening statement in these verses; namely, 'Lord, have we not prophesied … and done many wonders in Your name?' (Matthew 7:22). The mistaken assumption comes in the guise of 'works'. Relationship is defined by who we are, not what we do. Jesus did everything through and with the empowering Holy Spirit, in full communion with His Father. He did things *with* and not *for*. Likewise, we are called to do things with and not for God (whether in His name or on His behalf).

The mission we are called to, as His disciples, stems from a

---

[93] John 5:19; John 6:38.

place of relationship with God, to be at work where He is at work. Apart from that, what we engage in becomes 'good works' rather than 'God works'. We are to 'be about [our] Father's business' as Jesus was (Luke 2:49). The world does good works and often does them very well, and we can fall into the trap of believing wrongly that we are justified before God by what we do.

Our ministries, which incidentally are not ours but His, are a response to our love for Jesus and what He does through and in us, not a justification for being loved by Him. He has already accomplished everything on the cross to justify us before God. We can add nothing to that, but rather need to recognise His sacrifice, to receive it and respond to it.

This is the rock-solid nature on which we grow in our relationship with God: knowing Him and being known by Him. 'Therefore whoever hears these sayings of Mine, and does them, I will liken him to a wise man who built his house on the rock' (Matthew 7:24).

Do you know why the buildings in New York are taller than the buildings in London? Apart from the fact that everything is bigger in America – or so I'm told, never having been there – New York, as I understand, stands on rock, whereas London stands on clay. It means in New York there is firmer ground as a foundation on which to build. As such you can build higher and have greater stability.

The Rock on which our faith stands is Jesus Christ, and specifically our relationship with Him. The storms cannot separate those who are deeply rooted in relationship with Jesus, firmly planted on the Rock on which we are imbedded; inseparable and strong. This is the essence of securing that strong foundation in our lives that affects every aspect of who we are and how we live. He is the only Rock, the only anchorage that brings stability, direction, strength and meaning to our lives. Whatever life throws at us, we are secure because of Him:

> As you therefore have received Christ Jesus the Lord, so

> walk in Him, rooted and built up in Him and established in the faith, as you have been taught, abounding in it with thanksgiving.
> *Colossians 2:6-7*

It is here that being part of a church fellowship, where we remain firm and sure-footed, is so crucial. The world likes to propagate faith as being an individualistic experience of personal choice. But to follow Christ is a corporate encounter because we are one body in Him. Living in a loving and forgiving community is essential. It is in encouraging one another, supporting each other and growing together that we not only ourselves mature in that relationship, but facilitate others to do so as well. Coals only remain red-hot when they are in a burning hearth. Take a coal out of the hearth and place it on the side and it quickly grows cold; its glow and heat diminish. It is the same with the body of Christ. We can only thrive and be effective when we are part of and immersed in fellowship with one another and with Christ. When we isolate ourselves or become isolated through external means, we quickly grow cold. I often hear people who have backslidden and moved away from church involvement and fellowship say that they will come back; they're just taking time out. But the longer they remain separated, the less likely they are to return, and their faith, depending on their reasons for leaving, could eventually evaporate and die.

We are an interdependent community, not an independent gathering. It is this more than anything that enables us to remain sure-footed and confidently rooted in the face of persecution, whether from external opposition or internal complacency and indifference.

We continue to be the people Jesus has called to follow Him; gathered to walk with Him in unity and purpose; directed and empowered by His Holy Spirit to engage with a lost world; breaking the strongholds of indifference and opposition, and bringing hope and meaning that is real and life-enhancing. In so doing, we seek to extend His kingdom and, in the process, draw others to His love so they too may follow, as we do.

Thought break

- How willing are you to stand in His truth when faced with conflict? How do you react/respond when you hear/witness something that you know compromises your faith? What are the things that threaten your faith in Jesus?

- If you are confident that you are standing on solid rock, what are you building in your life that reflects or complements that assurance? How well do you think Jesus knows you?

- Think about the church fellowship you belong to. What do you most appreciate about it regarding your own journey of discipleship? If you are not part of a church fellowship, what aspects would most draw you to becoming part of one?

16

Heartfelt Treasure

What are the foundations or securities on which you build your life; the things you rely on or put your trust in? We may be able to cite all kinds of responses, but how valid and genuine they are becomes evident when we further ask whether we could do without them. But the essential question lies in whether we can do without God. When we take away our relationship with Him, we are left with living in the world on its terms.

Materialism and earthly wealth are very fickle and transient. I would go so far as to say there is no such thing as earthly security, because it is so unstable and unpredictable. A housing boom today is a housing crisis tomorrow. A stock market growth today is an economic crash tomorrow. A stable and secure job today is a redundancy tomorrow. Pension schemes that you spend your whole life putting into as a nest egg for retirement are lost, or no longer pay the expected dividend. The list goes on.

Putting all our trust in such securities can be foolhardy and unwise because this world carries so many uncertainties. Everything material has a sell-by date or an expiry date. Things have a limited shelf life. They eventually wear out, break down or decay and rot.

In addition, covetousness may feed our human desires and rob us of satisfaction because they can never fulfil what they promise. Here too there is vulnerability in what we possess. 'Do not lay up for yourselves treasures on earth, where moth and rust destroy and where thieves break in and steal' (Matthew 6:19). We should not put our hope in riches, acquisitions or possessions, for they cannot bring us security or deliverance. Values change and our earthly riches are only as good as the current financial climate says they are. 'Here today, gone tomorrow' is a familiar saying, but it is also a reality, and when we treat these earthly securities as our treasures, we are at risk of disappointment, disillusionment and regret. For some it can even be life-destroying.

Yet we live in a world that relies on many of these things for our everyday needs and requirements. It is worth pointing out here that Jesus is not prohibiting material possessions, nor the need or enjoyment of them. But He does warn us against creating ties that bind us to this earth in the self-centred or extravagant materialism that can preoccupy our lives.

The key issue concerns where our hearts are to be found. Are they in the underlying things that should be most important to us as His disciples? As we focus on our relationship with God, the important question arising should be how this affects our intimacy with and trust in our heavenly Father: 'For where your treasure is, there your heart will be also' (Matthew 6:21).

Our priorities underpin our focus and give precedence to that which is most precious to us. If we put our wholehearted trust in God, there our commitment will lie and there the source of our faith will empower us and mature us in our walk of discipleship. If our ties lie elsewhere, then so does our allegiance and, consequently, our devotion to Christ will waver.

How often do we become complacent with or indifferent to the richness of the life we have, and take for granted what is in front of us, while looking for satisfaction elsewhere? We can chase after dreams and illusions and in the end discover they bring nothing of worth. How many of us have been there and experienced that? How often have we been left disillusioned? Our real treasure lies not in the wealth we possess, whether material or spiritual, but in the One who gives it. It is God

Himself who is our 'delight' (Psalm 37:4). It is His presence that we are to seek after. Our most significant treasure is our relationship with Him, because only He can satisfy our deepest need, which is His reconciling love, enabling us to know His hope, peace and joy.

We have an 'inheritance' here and now when we place our trust in Jesus as our Saviour (Ephesians 1:11). The treasure Jesus speaks of is not restricted to an eternal inheritance we will receive when we are in glory with Him after we die. Remember, Jesus taught us to pray that it may be 'on earth as *it is in heaven*' (Matthew 6:10). We are encouraged to bring heaven to earth in our witness and outworking of faith. The presence of heaven is found only in Jesus, the One through whom our lives have fullness of meaning and direction. This is surely the 'treasure' we are to seek after (Matthew 13:44).

We need to remind ourselves that we have been called by the One who came to redeem us, reconcile us and restore us. It is Him that we follow. It is He who transforms us. We become a 'new creation' when we choose to say 'yes' to His invitation (2 Corinthians 5:17). Our walk with Him is one of intimacy, a relationship that empowers us to live in the fullness of life He brings us. It profoundly portrays the depth of God's love for us and underlines the fact that God is so passionately for us.

Whatever our circumstances, whatever we are going through, whatever others speak negatively over us, whatever the world presses us with, whatever our health issues, or financial issues, or relational issues, whatever we have messed up: none of it changes the fact that He is for us, always was and always will be. This is the heart of a loving Father who will go to whatever lengths are required to ensure we do not spend an eternity separated from His presence. He ultimately allowed His only begotten Son, Jesus, to take our place of shame and condemnation, to die rejected and isolated so we do not have to. It cost Him everything.

For the one who puts their total trust in Jesus, whose focus is kingdom-centred and whose relationship with God is such as to set our Father's priorities as their own, the resources of heaven are at their disposal. The riches of a heavenly inheritance are accessible here and now for the disciple who walks in nearness to their Lord, moment by moment, on the path set before them.

However, we must not assume that in our walk of following, we are immune to the pulls and enticements of a world that would lure us away from such a commitment. Jesus powerfully illustrated the temptations we are under, and how easily and unwittingly we can succumb, when He told the story of the prodigal son, who chose to take His inheritance and squander it in following earthly desires and pursuits, wastefully throwing away everything in the process (Luke 15:11-32). He had it all and then he lost it all.

We can sometimes fail to realise where our real treasure lies. We can squander or lose who we are and the true value of what we possess without necessarily realising what is slipping away from our grasp. The ways of the world we live in and the lifestyle we surround ourselves with can encroach on our inherited identity to the extent that our discipleship becomes an appendage, and our steadfastness in following Jesus evaporates into indifference or complacency. Our families, our work commitments, other pulls or pressing priorities then take centre stage, and the person we are called to be is left compromised and robbed of the most precious thing they possess.

The son in the story may have returned home for any number of reasons. Perhaps he realised he got it wrong and, missing what he had left behind, came to his senses. Or maybe he found himself in such an impoverished and destitute state, anything would have been preferable, and desperation dictated his ensuing actions of returning home. It is here that we see Jesus unfold the significance of what is at stake, what has been lost and what He wants to restore to us.

'And he arose and came to his father. But when he was still a great way off, his father saw him and had compassion, and ran and fell on his neck and kissed him' (Luke 15:20). Unashamedly, unreservedly, without waiting for explanations from his son or demanding an accounting for his rebellious actions, this father throws everything to one side and his only focus is to run to his son and throw his arms around him. What follows is so beautiful. The father not only welcomes the son home with open arms, but then also fully restores him to his former position. 'But the father said to his servants, "Bring out the best robe and put *it* on him, and put a ring on his hand and sandals on *his* feet"' (Luke 15:22).

The fact that his father looked to reclothe his son and reinstate him points to the reality that this young man stood before him with nothing. He was helpless, disempowered and no doubt feeling worthless as his father wrapped his loving, forgiving and reconciliatory arms around his son's trembling and impoverished frame. I would suggest, as I reflect on this fatherly response, that in his self-centred and self-seeking time away, the son had lost his identity, his authority and his purpose.

It is these three areas, portrayed by the depiction of being reclothed in the finest robe, the ring and the sandals, that we find the primary focus of our transformation when we are reconciled to Christ and choose to follow Him. We come to Him with nothing and receive everything, poured out upon us through His grace and mercy.

First, He gives us a new identity. We are clothed with Christ and henceforth belong to Him:

> I will greatly rejoice in the LORD,
> My soul shall be joyful in my God;
> For He has clothed me with the garments of salvation,
> He has covered me with the robe of righteousness,
> As a bridegroom decks *himself* with ornaments,
> And as a bride adorns *herself* with her jewels.
> *Isaiah 61:10*

What a wonderful image and truth. We are adorned in a beautiful garment called 'salvation'. Jesus is our salvation. It is the best robe we could ever wear. It is a top-of-the-range, priceless garment, with a designer label marked 'Calvary' and put together with a cross-stitch. It is a perfect fit. He took on our shame and guilt and instead clothed us in His righteousness. Our lives only have meaning in Jesus. He is our identity. We are forgiven, we are restored, we are healed. The old is arrayed in the new and is swallowed up, renewed and immersed in the intimacy of God's everlasting love. That is who we are. That is our uniqueness, not only in our calling but also in the nature that we take on and the expectations we embrace. It is for this and to this that He called us when He said, 'Follow Me.'

Second, He gives us a 'ring of authority', empowering us by His Holy Spirit to live as overcomers; to be environment-changers, filling the atmosphere with the presence of His kingdom. 'Yet in all these things we are more than conquerors through Him who loved us' (Romans 8:37). We are no longer orphans, but children of God, 'heirs with Christ' (Romans 8:16-17). We have status in Him. We are seated with Christ 'in the heavenly *places*' (Ephesians 2:6), the One to whom all authority has been given and who reigns far above everything in His created world. He has no equal in this or any other matter. And in His sovereignty, we walk with Him over all our circumstances, because His indwelling presence is constantly with us.

My understanding is that, as heirs and co-heirs with Christ, we have unlimited access to the resources of heaven at our disposal when we choose to follow Him and extend His kingdom in all He leads us in.[94] In Christ we are not powerless, nor are we to be intimidated by the worldly whispers that would seek to persuade us otherwise, that we are nothing and of no consequence.

Not only are we called and commissioned to do everything He did, but 'greater' things as well (John 14:12). All authority belongs to Him and therefore, by default of our relationship with Him, it is given to each one of us. It is through and in the

---

[94] John 14:13-14.

power of His Holy Spirit that we have confidence to press in and release that which is in us.

If this, then, is our identity and our authority in Christ, the third thing we receive as disciples is purpose. In Jesus' story, the son's only perceived hope when he returned was to become a servant, a hired hand. He would have settled for that, expecting nothing more. Even that would have been more than he had at that point in his messed-up life.

I wonder how many believers in Jesus at times see themselves similarly, as simply servants, devoting their time and energies to taking on roles in church rotas and activities, expecting little more than being part of a fellowship with little or no significant influence, impact or vision. I have often said, and repeat here, that God has a purpose for our lives greater than we could possibly imagine or think.[95] We have been called to serve, yes. But not from the status of a servant.

The son came to his father bare-footed and had sandals put on his feet. Why is that significant? Servants did not wear anything on their feet, whereas heirs did. The difference in terms of discipleship couldn't be more striking:

> No longer do I call you servants, for a servant does not know what his master is doing; but I have called you friends, for all things that I heard from My Father I have made known to you.
> *John 15:15*

Our faith in Jesus is not a blind faith. We do not hang around like a servant waiting to be told, 'Do this,' or, 'Do that.' We have been drawn into the intimate confidence of knowing and sharing in what our heavenly Father is doing. We are in conversation with Him regarding His will and purpose for our lives, the vision He instils in us as we journey with Him. Jesus makes that possible. His Holy Spirit instigates it. A servant goes *for* their master. A disciple goes *with* their beloved friend. He lets

---

[95] Ephesians 3:20.

us in on His thoughts and His plans.

It is here we discover His purpose for our lives, and it is here we are released into that purpose. We no longer travel empty-handed but are equipped for everything we are called to engage in, with every gift and resource necessary to see His kingdom having an impact on our communities, touching the lives of those we build relationships with and witness to. We are called to intimacy with the King of kings and Lord of lords. And there is more.

Because our identity is in Christ, our authority is in Christ and our purpose is in Christ, we are empowered to journey with intent and confidence, not anxiety, fear and intimidation. That is because we are also clothed in the peace of Christ. Jesus, the Prince of Peace, leaves His peace with us.[96] David Runcorn explains it like this: 'The peace of Jesus is not the absence of something but the presence of someone. It is a gift in the midst of life at its most burdened and stressful, not an escape from it.'[97]

It is not like any kind of peace the world can understand, let alone possess. Jesus therefore tells us not to be troubled, anxious or afraid: 'These things I have spoken to you, that in Me you may have peace. In the world you will have tribulation; but be of good cheer, I have overcome the world' (John 16:33). We are not only indwelt with His peace, but we are also peace carriers for others to receive. What is in you shapes what is around you. We wear the shoes of the 'gospel of peace' (Ephesians 6:15), called to bring His reconciliatory love into the troubled, fearful and hostile environments we find ourselves in. His peace changes the atmosphere around us because He has overcome the world and through us releases His *shalom*, the presence of who He is in the midst of where we are.

---

[96] John 14:27.
[97] David Runcorn, *Dust & Glory: Daily Bible Readings from Ash Wednesday to Easter Day* (Abingdon: Bible Reading Fellowship, 2015), p79.

In following Him

There is no substitute in any person's spirit for the knowledge of who they are in Christ; that their life has purpose and meaning; that they have a worth and are valued; that they are loved. There is nothing this world can offer that even comes close. There is nothing this world can do to separate us from such love, whatever it throws our way or entices us with.[98]

When we undertake this journey with Jesus, it becomes a road of encounter, of enterprise, of intrigue. Like all disciples who have gone before, we discover a greater understanding of who He is, but also who we are, transformed every day to be more and more like Him.

There will be times of excitement, encouragement and advancement as well as times of uncertainty, bewilderment and even disbelief at what He accomplishes in and through us. He continually raises our bar of anticipation and expectation to unimaginable heights. He fills our ordinary with His extraordinary in often surprising and unexpected ways. He goes ahead of us, preparing the way, and then walks with us, directing our path as we travel; sharing, conversing, absorbing, gathering, and building relationships as we go.

A fundamental question remains. Is God tugging at your heartstrings right now? Like those disciples on their way to Emmaus, in Luke 24, is there a fire stirring inside that is burning with passion, bursting out with a desire for more? We have come full circle, and the issue I raised at the start of this book returns. What kind of followers do we perceive ourselves to be? And perhaps more relevant, what kind of followers is Jesus calling us to become?

Because the transformation of following requires not only movement on our part, but also an ongoing re-evaluation and realignment of our lives as we journey with Him. What has changed or is changing in us becomes the litmus test of gauging

---

[98] Romans 8:38-39.

how far we have come. Are we willing to go where He takes us and to be prepared to follow where He leads? Or are we to be governed by our own agendas, institutional frameworks and religious observances, devoid of any meaningful intimacy with Him or obedience to His voice in His beckoning call, whereby He is heading in one direction and we in another?

Perhaps we have become so conditioned by a consumerist mentality in our approach to discipleship that we choose to keep Him at a safe distance, not getting too close, lest our comfort-zone approach to following disrupts our perceived spiritual equilibrium. If that is so, the danger is that we become separated from the embrace of His intimacy, His purpose and His will for our lives, and His *shalom* that envelops and indwells us.

In so doing, we end up following a hollow religious path devoid of the power and influence that is the very reason He has called us to engage with Him: to transform the lives of those around us in our communities and, in the process, to be ongoingly transformed ourselves. I'm not sure the lifeless tedium of such a religious path is what He has come to seek us out for. I'm not sure He sacrificed so much in order to reconcile us to Himself, restoring us in His image and likeness and renewing us in the fullness of the life He offers us, for us to simply 'sleepwalk' in the complacency of indifference and familiarity, in powerless comfort and convenience, with little or no impact on a lost and dying world that He came to save.

There is more. There must be. This is an invitation to come; come and see. Step out of the boat and into the storms of impossibility with the One who holds all things in His hand, whose natural environment breaks into the very places we fear to tread, and beckons us to follow.

Discipleship is a journey of those who are sent, commissioned to go with Him to every corner of this globe to make disciples, to baptise them 'in the name of Father ... Son and ... Holy Spirit' (Matthew 28:19), teaching and equipping them to grow into the maturity that brings the transformational encounter He desires. But to do that we have to abandon the go-carts we have become so fond of and dependent upon and get behind the wheel of the vehicle He designed for such a journey.

In all this, one thing is certain. We have the privilege of being with the God of all creation in close relationship with Him. He is never far away; in fact, closer that we could possibly imagine. We walk not with uncertainty but with assurance, on transformational pathways of promise. He says, 'Follow Me.' Will you?

Thought break

- What are the things you place your security in and how valid do you think they are? How effectively are you investing in heavenly treasures?

- Consider the story of the prodigal son. How much and in what ways might you identify with him?

- Reflect on your identity, authority and purpose in Christ. Are any of these areas compromised by your lifestyle or worldly influences? What might need to change for you to grow in these three areas?

Also by Henry Pradella:

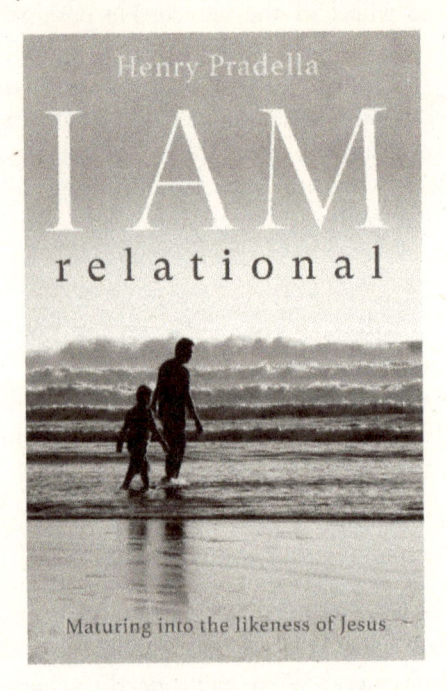

Henry Pradella
I AM
relational

Maturing into the likeness of Jesus

We are relational beings made in the image of a relational God.

In our fast-changing and increasingly pressured world, we can easily lose sight of who we are and what we were created for. Yet grasping our core relational identity as children of God and maturing into deeper relationship with Him – and one another – are fundamental to our discipleship and well-being.

I AM Relational is a rich blend of biblical teaching, personal insights and heartfelt testimonies that invite us into a journey of discovery and encounter. Tried and tested, its vibrant message will see new and seasoned believers alike maturing into life-changing experiences of the love of God and the relational likeness of Jesus.

You have an eternal place of belonging and an eternal relational purpose – are you ready to experience them?